OLD SHIRBURNIAN
NAVY & ARMY
LIST,
1914–1919.

SHERBORNE :
F. BENNETT AND CO., LTD., PRINTERS
MCMXXI.

PREFACE

TO THE
THIRD AND FINAL EDITION.

—

IT is more than five years since the
Second Edition of this Roll of Service and Honour was issued, and
more than three since the Armistice,
which was the beginning of the end of
the War,—that end which even now is
not fulfilled. Such blame as is due for
this delay I must take to myself : with
greater energy and method I should
have completed the work long ago, or,
better still, have caused it to be completed. I believe, however, that my
brother Shirburnians will with their
usual kindness be to my faults a little
blind, especially when they consider the
perplexities of these years and the mul-
tiplicity of duties laid upon me by the
vigorous development of the School.
The difficulty of collecting the mass of
facts which are here represented in a
much abbreviated form can only be
appreciated by those who have undertaken similar compilations. Very little
of the actual labour has been mine.
The first stage of preparing the original

Corpus of this Edition was kindly undertaken by Mr. Walter Lloyd, o.s., who made a card index of all the names and relevant facts that he could collect. The later stages of editing and augmenting this material owe most, once more, to the devoted energy of Mr. P. A. Baker, my former Secretary, who was himself dangerously wounded in France in 1917. Among many other helpers, the chief thanks are due to Major Davis and Captain Bensly, D.S.O., and to Sergeant-Major Wood, particularly in regard to the Distinctions. My present Secretary, Mr. E. A. Gibbs, has also given me indispensable assistance. To all these, and to others too numerous to mention, I desire to express sincere gratitude, not only on my own behalf but still more on behalf of our Shirburnian brotherhood, which, as the fruit of their labours, possesses a record of inexhaustible interest to us all and, as we hope, of perennial inspiration to succeeding generations of Shirburnians.

It is inevitable that there should be some mistakes and omissions in such a list. For any that were avoidable I ask pardon, only pleading that very great pains have been taken to make the list as correct and complete as possible. It is practically certain that no further edition will be printed: the cost of the present one far exceeds any sum that will be realised from the sale of copies. But any corrections will be thankfully received, if addressed to

O.S. RECORDS,
SCHOOL HOUSE,
SHERBORNE, DORSET,

and will be noted in a special copy kept in the School Library.

NOWELL SMITH,
Headmaster.

December, 1921.

HOUSES.

School House *(a)*.

James', Curteis', Wood's, Whitehead's, Wildman's, Carey's *(b)*.

Tancock's, Wilson's, Dunkin's *(c)*.

Blanch's, Bell's, Bensly's, Tindall's *(d)*.

Hetherington's, Rhoades', Hodgson's, King's *(f)*.

Milford's, Ross's *(g)*.

Town *(T)*.

Preparatory *(Prep.)*.

SIGNS.

†=killed. The Roll of Honour is printed on pages 149, 150, 151, 152, 153, 154, 155.

*=decorated or mentioned in despatches. It is not necessary to print a separate list of these distinctions.

ADDENDA AND CORRIGENDA.

The following information was received too late for inclusion in the main list.

†ABBOT, Lieut. E. J. W.—read, ABBOTT.

ABBOT, Lieut. F. G. W.—read, ABBOTT; house *c*.

*ADAMS, Lieut.-Com. (Bt.Com.) B. F.—read, mentioned in despatches (twice); D.S.O.

*ANSTRUTHER, Capt. (a./Lieut.-Col.) P. N.—add, mentioned in despatches (twice).

*APPLIN, Major and Bt. Lieut.-Col. R.V.K,—add, mentioned for war services.

*BAIRD, Major R. E.—add, O.B.E.

BAKER, 2nd Lieut. A. M. S. ... 1913-17 *f*
Royal Garrison Artillery.

*BALL, Capt. E. P.—add, O.B.E.

*BARKER, Capt. R. E.—Kurdistan, 1918-20, not 1918-19.

BARTLETT, Lieut. H. G.—read, BARTLEET.

BEVAN, Sub-Lieut. B. B. ... 1910-11 *a*
R.N.R.

BEVEN, L.-Corpl. A. L. H. ... 1912-13 *g*
Tank Corps.

BLAKELEY, Lieut. H. P.—read, BLAKELY.

*BIRKS, a./Capt. (temp. Major) E. R.—read, mentioned in despatches (twice).

BOND, Lieut. Denys ... ... 1894-98 *a*
At Dartmouth till August, 1917; then served in Intelligence Division of the Admiralty War Staff with a Commission as Lieut. R.N.V.R. until end of war.

BRADFORD, W. G. ... ... 1902-9 *a*
No definite information, but believed Capt.
in Somerset Light Infantry.

*CAMPBELL-ORDE, Lieut. A. C. ... 1912-15 *a*
Mentioned for war services ; A.F.C.

*COLLINS, Major C. H. G. ... ... 1900 *T.*
D.C.L.I.; Staff Capt., Alexandria, 1915 ;
A.A.Q.M.G., 53rd Welsh Division, 1917 ;
D.A.A.G.,Northern Division, Army of the
Rhine, 1919 ; O.B.E.

CORKE, Lieut. T. D. ... ... 1907-9 *b*
R.M.C.,Sandhurst,1916; Lieut.,Middlesex
Regiment, 1919.

*DEACON, Bt. Lieut.-Col.H.R.G.—read, mentions in despatches (four times).

DE PASS, G.—correct initials G. V. A.

Dow, Sergt. W. I.—correct initials W. J.

*FARRER, Major E. R. B.—read, mentioned in despatches (thrice) ; O.B.E.

*FLACK,2nd Lieut.H.L.—correct rank Major.

FLOWER,Lieut.E.J.—correct dates,1911-14 *a*.

FLOWER, 2nd Lieut. W. M.—correct dates,
1913-16 *g*.

†FRASER, 2nd Lieut.V. A. D.—correct initials
O.A.D.

*FREEMAN, Major C. T.—D.S.C. not D.S.O.

†FOLEY, Pte. E. B. ... ... 1905 *a*
Pte. in Canadian Forces; served in France;
wounded, and prisoner in Germany for two
years : died from effects of wounds, 1921.

FRISBY, C. G. ... ... 1908-11 *b*
Joined up in East Africa ; invalided out ;
(rank and unit not known).

GARLAND, 2nd Lieut. E. A. ... 1912-16 *c*
Worcestershire Regiment.

*GIBBONS, 2nd Lieut. H.—add, M.C.

GILL, Major E. E. ... ... 1902-6 *a*

†GRIERSON, Lieut. S.D.—correct initials S.V.

*HOBSON, Capt. E. R. C.—add, D.F.C.

HOPKINS, J. G. H. ... ... 1905-8 *b*
2nd Rhodesian Regiment (rank not known).

*IREMONGER, Col. E. A.—C.B.E. not G.B.E.

*KEIR, Surgeon Comdr. W. W.—read, mentioned in despatches (thrice).

*LAMB, Major D. G.—add, mentioned for war services.

LEE, 2nd Lieut. C. J.—correct initials C. I.

†*LIMBERY, Capt. C. R.—read, mentioned in despatches (twice).

†*LIMBERY, Capt. K. T.—read, mentioned in despatches (twice).

*LUCAS, Lieut. D.—should be starred.

LUXTON, Gentleman Cadet A. R. 1914-18 *f*
R.M.C., Sandhurst, 1918.

MAYBURY, Cadet M.—correct initials L. M.

MILLAR, Lieut. J. G. ... 1906-11 *T.* attached *b*
Indian Army, 1/19th Punjabis, 1918.

*MOBERLEY, Bt. Lt.-Col. A. H.—read, MOBERLY.

MONCKTON, Lieut. J. P.—correct initials I. P.

*MOORE, Major C. G. H.—should be starred.

NICHOLS,2nd Lieut.W.N.—read, NICHOLLS; house *c* not *g*.

NORSWORTHY, Lieut. E. ... 1905-8 *f*
R.A.S.C.; served in France.

†PEARSON, Cadet C. R. ... ... 1901-3 *b*
Cadet in Merchant Service; accidentally killed on H.M.S.Thistle, December, 1914.

PETERSON, Midshipman G. F. ... 1913-17 *f*
R.N.C., Keyham; Midshipman, June, 1918, H.M.S. Revenge.

PIM, Flight Cadet I.M.—correct initials J.M.

POWELL, Rev. J. R.—read, Army Chaplains'
Department; attached 2/17th London Regiment, 60th Division Artillery; and Staffordshire Yeomanry in Palestine, 1917 to 1919.

*RICKETT, Major G. R.—read, Lieut.-Col. ;
R.A.M.C.(T.); R.M.O.,DorsetYeomanry,
1914 to 1915 ; O.C. No. 88 General Hospital, E.E.F., Cairo, 1915 to 1919 ; mentioned in despatches (thrice) ; O.B.E.

*SLOMAN, Brig.-Genl. H. S., D.S.O.—read,
mentioned in despatches; twice mentioned
for war services.

SMITH, Lieut. D. F.   1906-8   *b*
Royal Fusiliers, 22nd Bn.

STREATFIELD, 2nd Lieut. T. B. M.—read,
STREATFEILD.

†STUART-FRENCH (STUART), Major
C. H.   1881-2   *f*
Inniskilling Fusiliers ; D.A.Q.M.G. to
Gen. Burn Murdock ; died on active ser-
vice, December 23rd, 1916, of heart failure.

STUART-FRENCH (STUART), Major Pascoe
W. G., J.P. 1881-4   *f*
1914,Supt. of Cork Remount Depôt; 1915,
Capt.; 1917 to 1919, in France, as Major,
with Remounts.

TULLIS, Capt. G. D. E., M.B.   ... 1905-7   *c*
R.A.M.C.; temp. Lieut., December,1915 ;
Capt., 1916 ; served with 23rd Division
and 50th Casualty Clearing Station in
France and Flanders; demobilised,Decem-
ber, 1918.

*TURTON, Major M. S.—read, mentioned in
despatches (thrice).

WALSH, Col. H. A., C.B.—starred by mis-
take.

*WILSON, Capt. R. H.—add, M.C.

OLD SHIRBURNIAN NAVY & ARMY LIST

(ARRANGED ALPHABETICALLY).

*ABELL, Major C. F. 1902-4   *f*
R.N.V.R.(H.M. Air Service); Lieutenant,
R.N.V.R., attached R.N.A.S., May,1915;
promoted Lieut.-Comdr., R. N. V. R.,
December, 1917; transferred as Major
R.A.F., April, 1918; Military O.B.E.

*ABELL, Major G. H. 1900-3   *f*
R.N.V.R.; Lieutenant for engineering
duties R.N.A.S., August, 1915; promoted
Lieut.-Comdr., January,1917; transferred
to R.A.F. as Major (Technical), April,
1918; mentioned in despatches; O.B.E.

†ABBOT, Lieut. E. J. W. ... 1898-1903   *c*
The Royal Inniskilling Fusiliers, 2nd Bn.,
attached 4th Bn. (extra Reserve), and then
to Royal Irish Fusiliers; killed at Festubert
(or Richebourg), May 16th or 17th, 1915.

ABBOT, Lieut. F. G. W. ... 1903-4
Prince Albert's (Somerset Light Infantry),
8th Bn.; attached 9th (Reserve) Bn.;
transferred to 6th (S.) Bn.,B.E.F., France.

ADAMS, Sub-Lieut. N. ... ... 1908-12 *Prep.*
R.N.; H.M.S. Courageous.

ADAMS, Lieut. A. G. ... ... 1906-13*T.&g*

I.A.R.O.; on duty with the Burma Military Police in connection with the Kuki Punitive Measures Force, Chin Hills, Burma.

*ADAMS, Lieut.-Com. (Bt.Com.) B.F. 1900-2 *c*

H.M.S. Cumberland ; mentioned in despatches.

*ADAMS, Capt. G. H. ... ... 1901-4 *c*

Australian Field Artillery, 48th Batt. ; M.C.

ADAMS, Sub-Lieut. H. ... ... 1906-11 *Prep.*

R.N.; Served 1914, H.M.S. Emperor of India; 1916, H.M.S. Agincourt; 1918, was present in destroyer in attacks on Zeebrugge and Ostend.

ADAMS, Capt. H. R. ... ... 1906-10 *T.*

Honourable Artillery Company ; served April, 1915, with 1st (Infantry) Bn., Machine Gun Section (wounded at Hooge, June, 1915) ; and with 3rd (Infantry) Bn. in France from December, 1916, to December, 1917 ; Adjutant of 2/72nd Punjabis, Indian Army, February, 1918.

ADAMS, Lieut. O. P. ... ... 1908-13*T.&g*

R.F.A., 3/75th Brigade; served in France; and in Mesopotamia with 1/4th Bn. (T.), the Dorsetshire Regiment.

ADAMS, temp./Lieut.-Col. R. J. ... 1893-8 *T.*

Indian Army, Commanding 20th Bn., 131st United Provinces Regiment, previously in Indian Police.

†ADAMSON, Capt. W. ... 1899-1903 *a*
The Loyal North Lancashire Regiment,
11th (Reserve) Bn.; killed in Mesopotamia,
April 23rd or 24th, 1916.

ADAMTHWAITE, 2nd Lieut. J.W. E. 1906-9 *c*
Royal Army Service Corps, 2nd Notts
and Derby Mounted Brigade.

ADDINGTON, Major W. L. ... 1868-71 *b*
The Queen's (Royal West Surrey) Regiment (Ret. pay); employed at Depôt,
'The Queen's' Regiment, September,
1914, to January, 1918.

ADDISON, J. F. P. ... ... 1903-4 *b*
Cyclist Corps and R.N. Division (Anson
Bn.); served in France; wounded.

ADYE, Capt. L. C. ... ... 1907-11 *c*
The Duke of Wellington's (West Riding
Regiment), 3rd Bn. (Reserve); attached
2nd Bn.; gas poisoned May 5th, 1915;
wounded July 1st, 1916; non-combatant
from May 5th, 1917.

AGAR, Pte. B. M. S. ... ... 1909-13 *b*
The Royal Fusiliers (City of London
Regiment), Public Schools Bn.

AINSLIE, Sub-Lieut. W. St. J. ... 1909-12 *Prep.*
R.N.; Served on H.M.S. Queen Eliza-
beth from May, 1917, to Armistice.

†ALDERSON, Capt. A. G. J. ... 1914-16 *Master*
The Duke of Cornwall's Light Infantry,
2/5th Bn. (T.); Lieutenant, Machine
Gun Corps; killed in accident during
bombing practice at Grantham, October
19th, 1916.

ALEXANDER, Lieut. K. E. ... 1911-16   *g*
The Durham Light Infantry, 2nd Bn.;
served in France; severely wounded and
taken prisoner March 21st, 1918; reached
home January 4th, 1919; demobilized,
April 17th, 1919; Special Reserve of
Officers.

ANDERSON, Col. R. F. H. ... 1872-7   *a*
(Indian Army, Retired) Assistant Provost
Marshal, Q.M.G., 17th Division.

ANDERSON, Lieut. W. H. ... 1902-3   *b*
The Gloucestershire Regiment, 1/6th Bn.
(T.).

ANSON, 2nd Lieut. C. O. ... 1914-17   *a*
Royal Air Force, R.A.F. Station, Fowl-
mere, Royston, Herts.

*ANSTRUTHER, Capt. (a./Lieut.-Col.)
P. N. 1905-9   *d*
The Queen's Own (Royal West Kent)
Regiment, 2nd Bn.; Adjt. 7th (S.) Bn.;
D.S.O., M.C.

*APLIN, Bt. Col. P. J. H. ... 1873-6   *a*
Indian Army, 1st Class Interpreter; Com-
manding 18th (S.) Bn. (1st Public Works,
Pioneers), The Duke of Cambridge's
Own (Middlesex Regiment); D.S.O.

*APPLIN, Major and Bt. Lieut.-Col. R.
V. K. 1883-6   *a*
14th Hussars; Instructor, Machine Gun
Corps Training Centre, July, 1916, to
October, 1917; mentioned in despatches;
D.S.O.

†Armstrong, Lieut.-Col. C. A. ... 1888-9 *f*
The Northumberland Fusiliers ; 2nd in
Command, 8th (S.) Bn. ; killed in France,
October 1st, 1915.

†Awdry, Lieut. W. W. ... ... 1911-14 *d*
The Duke of Edinburgh's (Wiltshire
Regiment) ; died, April 14th, 1918, of
wounds received same day near Kemmell
Hill.

†Bacchus, Capt. and Adjt.W. H. O. 1901-2 *a*
The York and Lancaster Regiment, 1st
Bn. ; died September 13th, 1915, of
wounds received in Flanders.

*Back, Capt. G. A., M.B. (Camb.) 1906-10 *a*
R.A.M.C. ; served in France, Mesopotamia and Persia; mentioned in despatches.

*Baddeley, Capt. S. E. L. ... 1900-4 *a*
19th Lancers (Fane's House), Indian
Army ; served in France with the Indian
Contingents ; from February, 1918, with
the Egyptian Expeditionary Force ; mentioned in despatches.

Bailey, Capt. C. H. ... ... 1910-12 *d*
The Monmouthshire Regiment, 1st Bn. ;
resigned through ill-health, March, 1916.

Baird, Major R. E. ... ... 1892-7 *a*
The Highland Light Infantry ; attached
1st Garrison Bn., Royal Scots Fusiliers.

†Baker, Capt. C. D. ... ... 1886-9 *Price*
Grenadier Guards (Special Reserve) ;
attached 1st Bn. ; killed in France, July
29th, 1917.

*BAKER, Lieut.-Col. E. E. F.   ... 1908-14   *f*
The Duke of Cambridge's Own (Middlesex Regiment), 5th Bn., attached 2nd Bn.; mentioned in despatches (twice); M.C. with bar; D.S.O.

†BAKER, 2nd Lieut. G. L. J.   ... 1910-15   *f*
Middlesex Regiment; killed in action, 28th April, 1917.

*BAKEWELL, Lieut. (a./Major)W. B. 1908-13   *f*
The Queen's Own (Royal West Kent Regiment), 5th Bn. (T.); seconded, Machine Gun Corps, 286th Coy., Abbottabad, N.W.F.P., India; mentioned in despatches.

BALL, Capt. E. P.   ...   1905-1905   *d*
110th Mahratta Light Infantry.

†BAMFORD, Pte. A.   1903-5   *f*
Grenadier Guards; killed, near Loos, October 11th, 1915.

*BAMFORD, Bt. Major E. 1900-2   *T.*
Royal Marine Light Infantry, H.M.S. Royal Sovereign; mentioned in despatches; V.C., D.S.O.; Order of St. Anne, 3rd Class (Russian); Légion d'Honneur.

BAMFORD, Lieut. R. 1897-1900   *T.*
Royal Army Service Corps, Mechanical Transport; served one year as private in The London Regiment, 25th (County of London) Cyclist Bn.; in France from November, 1915.

BARCLAY, Sergt. W. E. A.   ... 1901-6   *b*
Canadian Gordon Highlanders.

7

BARCLAY, Paymaster-Lieut. J. C. H. 1907-10 *b*
H.M.S. Hercules.

*BARDSWELL, Major N. D., M.D., F.R.C.P.,
F.R.S. (Edin.) ... ... 1886-9 *c*
R.A.M.C. Service:—Netley Hospital;
Mediterranean E.F.(O.C. MaltaR.A.M.C.
detachment for duty in Sicily, 1915);
Hospital Ship 'Britannic'; B.E.F.,
France; M.V.O.

*BARKER, Capt. R. E. ... ... 1904-7 *d*
The Prince of Wales's Volunteers (South
Lancashire Regiment), 1st Bn.; attached
33rd Signal Company, Mesopotamia E.F.,
1916-18; mentioned in despatches(thrice);
special employ, Kurdistan, Persia, 1918;
Political, Kurdistan, 1918-19.

†BARNES,2nd Lieut. (a./Capt.) J.E.T. 1907-13 *f*
The Gloucester Regiment, 7th (S.) Bn.;
served in Gallipoli (August, 1915), in
Egypt, and in the attempted relief of Kut;
killed, 3rd February, 1917, in Mesopotamia.

BARNES, Major S. F. ... ... 1903-7 *a*
Territorial Force Reserve; Royal Garri-
son Artillery, 3rd (Portland) Company,
Dorsetshire R.G.A.; coast defence, Port-
land, August, 1914, to March, 1916; then,
B.E.F., France, with 123rd Siege Battery,
R.G.A., to April, 1917; 502nd Siege
Battery, R.G.A., September, 1917, to
February, 1918; then posted to No. 2
S.A.R.B.; G.S., November, 1918.

†BARRY, Capt. N. J. M. ... 1898-1900 *c*
East African Transport Corps; killed in
German East Africa, October 21st, 1917.

BARTER, Lieut. C. M. 1912-16   *g*
Royal Air Force; 44th, 49th and 51st
Foreign Squadrons.

BARTLETT, Lieut. H. G. ... 1906-9   *c*
The Essex Regiment, 3rd Bn. (Special
Reserve); attached 1st Bn.; acting Adjt.
on Peninsular from October to December,
1915; wounded at Beaumont Hamel,
August, 1916; invalided out, January,
1918.

BARTLETT, Corpl. E. P. ... 1910-12   *d*
The Dorsetshire Regiment, 2/4th Bn. (T.).

*BARTON, Capt. H. G. M. ... 1897-9   *d*
Royal Engineers; mentioned in despatches.

BASEVI, Lieut.-Col. W. H. ... 1877-80   *a*
Army Pay Department; Staff Paymaster,
Base VI.

BASHALL, Corpl. W. H. 1901-5   *a*
83rd Company M.T., Royal Army Service
Corps, B.E.F.

BASHALL, Corpl. J. T. 1904-6   *a*
83rd Company M.T., Royal Army Service Corps, B.E.F.

*BASS-THOMSON, Lieut. L. D. ... 1897-1901   *b*
R.N.V.R., Motor Boat Reserve; Légion
d'Honneur; Order of the White Eagle
(Serbian); Order of the Crown of Italy;
and the Croix de Guerre.

BATHURST, Major A. H. (Retired) 1886-90   *a*
Dep. Asst. Adjt. Gen., Eastern Command.

BATHURST, Capt. C., M.P. ... 1883-6   *a*
Royal Engineers (Special Reserve), R.
Monmouthshire; Asst. Military Secretary,
S. Command.

†BATTERSBY, Capt. E. M. ... 1899-1901   *d*
The Queen's Own (Royal West Kent
Regiment), 3rd Bn.; killed at Neuve
Chapelle, October 27th, 1914.

*BATTISHILL, Lieut. P. H. ... 1903-7   *d*
The Prince of Wales's Own (West Yorkshire Regiment), 4th Bn.; wounded, July
28th, 1918; M.C. and Bar.

†BAWDON, 2nd Lieut. R. H. ... 1909-13   *f*
The South Wales Borderers, 7th (S.) Bn.;
died on Active Service, July 10th, 1915.

BAX, Cadet S. N. 1913-18   *c*
Officers Cadet Bn., Household Brigade.

*BAXTER, Capt. (a./Major) D. ... 1906-10   *b*
The Gloucester Regt, 1st Bn.; seriously
wounded 1st battle of Ypres, October,
1914; attached Machine Gun Corps (1918),
14th Bn.; M.C.; mentioned in despatches
(twice).

BAYLISS, Lieut. A. W. E. ... 1907-9   *a*
Royal Engineers (Territorial Force); 69th
Div. Sig. Co., E. Anglian.

†BAYLY, 2nd Lieut. V. T. ... 1910-12   *d*
The Dorsetshire Regiment, 7th (S.) Bn.;
killed, near Albert, May 7th, 1916.

BEADON, Naval Cadet R. ... 1913-16 *Prep.*
Osborne, 1916; Dartmouth, 1917, to
Armistice.

BEALE, Sergt. C. W. ... ... 1901-2 *b*
Royal Air Force.

†BEAN, Lieut. C. R. C. ... ... 1905-8 *b*
The South Staffordshire Regt. ; killed,
near Ypres, October 26th, 1914.

*BECKETT, Capt. W. E.... ... 1910-14 *c*
The Cheshire Regiment, 3rd Bn. ; mentioned in despatches ; G.S.O. 3rd Grade,
27th Division.

†*BECKTON, Lieut. H. ... ... 1907-11 *d*
Royal Field Artillery ; died 23rd Septem-
ber, 1919, of illness as a result of wounds ;
Croix de Guerre.

BECKTON, S./Sergt. H. S. ... 1906-10 *b*
16th Canadian Infantry Bn. (Canadian
Scottish) ; wounded April, 1915 ; transferred to Canadian Pay and Record Office.

BELL, 2nd Lieut. C. D. ... ... 1905-7 *f*
The Northumberland Fusiliers.

BELLAIRS, Lieut. I. M. ... 1897-1900 *f*
R.N.A.S., 10th August, 1914 ; served in
France and Belgium ; Secret Service in
Holland and Germany ; 1916 and 1917,
East Africa.

†BENBOW, Pte. J. L. ... ... 1902-5 *b*
The Royal Fusiliers (City of London
Regiment) ; killed in action, at the attack
on Combles, September 15th, 1916.

†BENISON, 2nd Lieut. E. W. ... 1903-8 *a*
Royal Garrison Artillery (T.), No. 3
Company, Dorsetshire ; died of peritonitis
at Weymouth, August 13th, 1915.

*BENET, Lieut.-Col. H. V. F. ... 1876-9   *b*
  Lancashire Fusiliers (Reserve of Officers);
  G.S.O., 2nd Grade, War Office; C.B.E;
  Légion d'Honneur, Croix d'Officier;
  Order of St. Valdimir, 4th Class with
  swords and bow; of St. Stanislaus, 2nd
  Class with swords; of St. Anne, 2nd Class
  with swords.

BENNET, Col. F. W. 1862-7   *a*
  Royal Engineers.

BENNETT, Pte. D. 1900-5   *a*
  Honourable Artillery Company, 1st Bn.

†BENNETT, Sergt. B. C. 1905-7   *d*
  Dorset Yeomanry (Queen's Own), 1st Bn.;
  killed in Palestine, May 4th, 1917.

*BENNETT, Capt. G. 1906-11   *a*
  Intelligence Corps (G.H.Q. Staff,France);
  formerly in Royal Army Service Corps;
  mentioned in despatches.

BENNETT, Capt. and Hon. Major L.
  W. 1880-3   *b*
  The Queen's (Royal West Surrey)
  Regiment, 9th (2nd Reserve) Bn.; em-
  ployed at Depôt, Suffolk Regiment.

*BENNETT, Lieut. M. C. ... 1903-6   *f*
  The Herefordshire Regiment, 1st Bn.;
  5th Company, Imp. Camel Corps, E.E.F.;
  mentioned in despatches.

†BENNETT, Lieut. M. P. ... 1911-15   *g*
  The Queen's (Royal West Surrey) Regiment, 2nd Bn.; died of wounds received
  near the Menin Road, October 8th, 1917.

*BENNETT, Capt. W. ... ... 1905-8 *a*
Royal Engineers; Signals, 9th Corps,
Heavy Artillery; M.C.

†BENNETTS, Flight Sub-Lieut. E. A. 1909-13 *c*
R.N.A.S.; Formerly Lance-Corpl. in
Cape Town Highlanders, South African
Defence Force (Signalling Instructor);
killed in an air battle, N.E. of Lens,
August 17th, 1917.

*BENSLY, Capt. (temp. Major) The) 1888-93 *a*
Rev. W. J. ... ...) 1905-*Master*
1st United Provinces Horse, India,
1914-15; 7th Bn., Dorsetshire Regiment,
1915-16; 1st Bn., West Indian Regiment,
1916-19; served in India, Egypt, Sinai
and Palestine; D.S.O.; mentioned in
despatches.

BENSON, 2nd Lieut. T. G. ... 1912-18 *f*
Kings Own Yorkshire Light Infantry.

BENSTED, Corpl. F. H. ... ... 1909-12 *c*
Royal Engineers; Motor Cycle Despatch
Rider, 28th Division, Signal Company;
invalided out.

BENSTED, Driver J. A. ... ... 1912-13 *c*
Honourable Artillery Company; (965)
2/1st 'B.' Battery, 126th Brigade, R.F.A.,
B.E.F.

*BENT, Lieut. H. K. R. ... ... 1911-13 *g*
Inns of Court O.T.C. and Royal Field
Artillery; served in France, gassed and
wounded; discharged permanently unfit,
March, 1918; M.C.

BERKELEY, Lieut. M. H. ... 1913-17 *c*
Indian Army; Ghurkha Rifles, 1/7th Bn.;
served in Persia.

BERRYMAN, Capt. F. H.   ... 1883-6   *a*
Royal Garrison Artillery (late Cardigan
R. F. Reserve, A.).

*BEST, Comdr. The Hon. M. R. ... 1887-90 *Prep.*
R.N. ; D.S.O., M.V.O.

BERTRAM, Capt. J. N.   1902-5   *f*
The Royal Scots (Lothian Regiment),
7th Bn.

*BESANT, Major R. E.   1896-8   *c*
Commandant, R. A. Reinforcement
Camp, Fifth Army, France ; previously
served as private in Universities and
Public Schools Bns., Royal Fusiliers ;
Commission in 10th (S.) Bn., Loyal North
Lancashire Regiment, October, 1914, to
April, 1916 ; D.T.M.O. attached to 37th
Divisional Artillery Staff to December,
1916; Chief Instructor, Trench Mortar
School, Fifth Army, to June, 1918 ; men-
tioned in despatches (thrice).

†BETTS, 2nd Lieut. C. C.   ... 1913-17   *c*
Royal Air Force ; killed, April 17th, 1918,
(in the Aegean Sea owing to engine
trouble) while on his way to bomb the
Goeben.

*BETTS, Capt. E. B. C.   ... 1911-14   *c*
Royal Air Force ; D.S.C., D.F.C. ; Croix
de Guerre with palms (French).

BEWES, 2nd Lieut. H. T.   ... 1901-6   *a*
The Dorsetshire Regiment, 3rd Bn.
(Reserve).

BIENEMAN, Rev. G. A. ...   1888-92 *Master*
Chaplain to 30th Casualty Clearing
Station.

BIRCH, Major D. P. L. 1877-9   a
Royal Garrison Artillery (Reserve of Officers).

*BIRD, Major A.   1869-72   d
R.A.M.C. (T.F.) ; O. i/c Troops, Ambulance Transport, St. Denis ; mentioned for War Services.

BIRD, Capt. C. E. H. 1904-5   a
Royal Army Service Corps ; O.C., R.A.S.S., 68th Brigade, Royal Garrison Artillery.

*BIRKS, a./Capt. (temp. Major) E. R. 1893-7   a
West Riding Brigade, R.F.A. (T.) ; O.C. 3/3rd Brigade, June 1st, 1915, to February 28th, 1916 ; C.R.O. 33rd Regimental District, June 1st, 1916, to March 25th, 1918 ; Overseas, May, 1918 ; commanding a P.O.W. Company in France since October, 1918 ; mentioned in despatches.

BITTLESTON, Lieut. D. H.   ... 1908-11 c&T.
R.F.A., ' A ' Battery, 88th Brigade ; served in France, September to November, 1915 ; with Salonika Force, November, 1915, to January, 1919.

BLACKMORE, Bombadier H. C.   ... 1884-90 Price
Royal Garrison Artillery.

†BLAIR, 2nd Lieut. G. Y.   ... 1908-13   b
R.F.A., 10th Division ; killed in France, July 24th, 1915.

BLAKELEY, Lieut. H. P.   ... 1914-16   g
Royal Air Force ; Cadet, April, 1917 ; 2nd Lieut., July, 1917 ; Lieutenant, March, 1918 ; France, 46th Squadron, October, 1917 ; Rochford (Essex), 61st Squadron, Home Defence, August, 1918 ; Demobilised, March, 1919.

†BLANDFORD, Pte. C. E. ... 1910-13 *a*
The King's Royal Rifle Corps, 22nd Bn.;
attached 5th Field Survey Bn., Royal
Engineers; killed in France, July 20th,
1918.

BLANDFORD, 2nd Lieut. J. V. ... 1913-15 *a*
Royal Air Force; on Active Service with
H.M.S. 'Royal Sovereign' in the North
Sea.

†BLENCOWE, Capt. E. C. B. ... 1896-9 *c*
The Dorsetshire Regiment, 6th (S.) Bn.;
killed on the Bluff, near Hill 60, Ypres
Salient, February 16th, 1916.

†BLIGH, 2nd Lieut. E. ... ... 1908-13 *f*
The East Lancashire Regiment, 3rd Bn.
(Reserve); attached 2nd Bn.; killed at
Fromelles, May 9th, 1915.

BLIGH, Capt. W., M.D., B.Sc. (Lond.),
M.R.C.S., L.R.C.P. ... 1880-4 *d*
R.A.M.C.; No. 9, Rouen, December,
1916 to September, 1917; No. 38,
Stationary, Genoa, August, 1918; then to
Caesar's Camp and No. 11, General,
Genoa.

*BOLTON, Lieut. E. J. ... ... 1910-15 *b*
The Dorsetshire Regiment, 3rd Bn.
(Reserve); attached 5th Bn.; M.C.

†BOND, Capt. C. G. ... 1892-1900 *a*
The Duke of Edinburgh's (Wiltshire
Regiment); Adjt. 1/4th Bn. (T.); killed
at Givenchy, November 25th, 1915.

*BOND, Lieut. E. F. ... ... 1900-5 *a*
111th Siege Battery, Royal Garrison
Artillery; M.C.

*BOND, Lieut.-Col. J. H. R. ... 1884-7   *c*
R.A.M.C.; mentioned in despatches
(thrice); C.B.E., D.S.O.

BOURKE, Lieut.-Col. H. B., D.S.O. 1871-2   *b*
West India Regiment; retired; (late
1st); served as Draft Conducting Officer.

*BOUSFIELD, Lieut.-Col. H. R. ... 1877-8   *a*
Retired, 1913; Chairman Durban
Recruiting Committee, 1914-18; Chair-
man Re-employment Soldier's Committee,
1917; Member Central Advisory Board,
(S.A.) Records and Re-employment,1918;
C.M.G.

BOWEN, Major A. G. W. ... 1876-80   *d*
Royal Army Medical Corps; Military
Convalescent Hospital, Crownhill Hut-
ments, near Plymouth.

†BOWEN, Lieut. E. G. A. ... 1907-11   *f*
On coast defence at outbreak of war;
went to Flanders with 71st Heavy Battery,
June, 1915; became Observer, in No. 6
Squadron, R.F.C., in August, 1915;
passed as Pilot, May, 1916, and joined
22nd Squadron on Somme front; killed,
fighting in the air, between Thilloy and
Le Barque, September 8th, 1916.

*BOWKER, Major W. J., D.S.O. ... 1880-5   *d*
Prince Albert's (Somerset Light Infantry),
2nd Bn.; C.M.G.

BOWMAN, Capt. J. H. ... 1897-1900   *b*
The Durham Light Infantry, 2/7th Bn.
(T.); also served with North Russian
Expeditionary Force, 1918-19.

*BOYD, Capt. J. E. M. 1889-91   *f*
Royal Army Medical Corps; M.C.

BOYNE, Capt. L. L.   1903-5   *c*
The Royal Sussex Regiment, 3rd Bn.
(Reserve).

*BRADFORD, Capt. and Adjt. J. P. ...   1900-2   *e*
Royal Army Service Corps, Base
Mechanical Transport Depôt (Northern),
France ; mentioned in despatches.

BRADFORD, Major L. B.   ... 1902-4   *c*
R.F.A. ; Dorsetshire Battery, 3rd Wessex
Brigade(T.); commanding 1103rd Battery,
227th Brigade, R.F.A., stationed at
Secunderabad, August, 1917 ; command-
ing 'A' Battery, 312th Brigade, R.F.A.,
62nd Division, B.E.F., France ; gassed,
September 17th, 1918.

BRAKSPEAR, Capt. A. R.   ... 1885-8   *a*
Oxford and Bucks Light Infantry, 4th Bn.;
invalided out, July, 1916.

BRAMALL, Capt. E. G. 1908-12   *f*
The Royal Sussex Regiment, 5th (Cinque
Ports) Bn. (T.).

BRAMALL, Major E. H. 1903-8   *f*
R.F.A.; served in Egypt; Staff Capt.,
19th Div. Artillery, April to July, 1916;
commanding D/86 Brigade, July to September, 1916; invalided home, September,
1916, to November, 1917 ; commanding
C/86 Brigade, November to February,
1918 ; invalided home, February, 1918 ;
attached Officer, A.G. 2 (O), War Office.

*BRASSEY, Capt. H. R. 1906-9   *c*
Royal Field Artillery, B/70th Brigade ;
M.C.

18

BRATBY, Lance-Corpl. G. S. ... 1892-4 *d*
The Gloucestershire Regiment, 3rd (S.)
Bn. ; gassed and shell shocked, July, 1916 ;
discharged, February, 1918.

*BRATBY, a./Capt. S. H. ... ... 1892-5 *d*
Royal Army Service Corps, 3/1st East
Lancashire Division ; served in Mesopotamia, October, 1916, to August, 1918 ;
mentioned in despatches (twice) ; M.B.E.

BREWIS, 2nd Lieut. E. ... ... 1913-16 *a*
Royal Army Service Corps.

BRIDGE, 2nd Lieut. D. E. ... 1902-3 *a*
H.Q., 402nd M.T. Company, Royal Army
Service Corps. Canadian Corps, Seige
Park, B.E.F.

BRIDGES, Major T. McG. ... 1886-90 *a*
The Loyal North Lancashire Regiment,
2nd Bn.

†BRINE, Lieut. E. L. ... ... 1905-9 *a*
The Hampshire Regiment, 3/4th Bn. ;
attached 1/4th Bn., Indian Expeditionary
Force ; served in Mesopotamia ; died of
enteric at Hamadam, Persia, September
24th, 1918.

BROADMEAD, Bt. Col. H. ... 1872-9 *a*
Essex Regiment.

†BROADRICK, Major F. B. D. ... 1881-4 *f*
R.F.A. ; died in hospital at Harve, April
19th, 1918.

†BROOKE, Capt. G. D. ... ... 1905-8 *c*
The Suffolk Regiment, 7th (S.) Bn. ;
killed, July 3rd, 1916, at Ovillers-la-Boiselle.

BROOKMAN, Capt. O. J. R. ... 1897-1900 *c*
Royal Army Service Corps; Mechanical
Transport.

BROOKS-KING, Lieut. M. ... 1908-13 *c*
Prince Albert's (Somerset Light Infantry),
2/5th Bn. (T.); served in India from
December, 1914; Signalling Officer to the
Brigade.

BROWN, Capt. B. W., M.B. ... 1899-1904 *T.*
R.A.M.C.

BROWN, Lieut. C. A. ... ... 1900-6 *T.*
R.F.A.

BROWN, Lieut. C. B. ... ... 1898-1904 *b*
Unattached List (T.F.); Christ's Hospital
O.T.C.

BROWN, 2nd Lieut. E. F. ... 1905-9 *d*
Royal Engineers; Railway Operative
Department; served in Salonika.

BROWN, Capt. I. A. ... ... 1905-9 *T.*
The Royal Warwickshire Regiment, 2nd
Bn.

†BROWN, Lieut. O. ... ... 1902-6 *T.*
4th (Royal Irish) Dragoon Guards;
attached from 7th Hariana Lancers;
killed in France. April 24th, 1915.

BROWN, 2nd Lieut. M. E. ... 1914-17 *g*
Royal Air Force; Cadet, October 3rd,
1917 (Wendover, St. Leonard's and
Hastings); 2nd Lieut., June, 1918;
France, 102 Squadron; Hospital, October,
1919; Demobilised, November, 1919.

BROWN, Lieut. W. F. ...   ... 19.14-16   *c*
Royal Military College, Sandhurst, and
18th (Q.M.O.) Hussars; Secunderabad,
India.

*BROWNE-MASON, Lieut.-Col. H.O.B. 1885-9   *a*
R.A.M.C.; taken prisoner at fall of Kut;
repatriated to India, September, 1916;
mentioned in despatches (twice); D.S.O.

BRUTTON, Major G. K. H.   ... 1882-5   *b*
Headquarters Chinese Labour Corps.

BUCHANAN, Lieut.-Col. J. B.W., M.B. 1877-8   *b*
R.A.M.C.

BUCHANAN-WOLLASTON, 2nd Lieut.
H. J.   1896-9   *a*
DorsetYeomanry (Queen's Own), 2nd Bn.

*BUCKLE, Major-Gen. C. R.   ... 1875-80   *c*
Royal Artillery; C.B., C.M.G., D.S.O.;
Légion d'Honneur, Order of Crown of
Italy, Order of Military Savoy, Order of
Leopold 1st, Order of Leopold 2nd, Croix
de Guerre; mentioned in despatches ten
times.

BUCK, Capt. F. C. W. 1906-7   *d*
Royal Army Service Corps; attached
93rd Brigade, R.G.A.; served in France
from December 28th, 1914.

BULL, Capt. W. R.   1902-7   *f*
Royal Army Service Corps.

*BULLEN, Lieut. D. B. F.   ... 1900-4   *c*
Canadian Infantry, 8th Bn. (90th Winni-
peg Rifles); mentioned in despatches.

BULLOCK, Lieut. J. C. C. ... 1913-16   *g*
18th King George's Own Lancers, Indian
Army, B.E.F., France.

BULLOCK, Lieut. P. C. 1914-17   *g*
Indian Army; Cadet College, Quetta;
14th Jat Lancers; O.C. Veterinary
Hospital, Bareilly.

BUNBURY, Major W. C. H. ... 1882-5   *a*
The Gordon Highlanders, 9th Bn.;
served at Depôt, Royal Scots (Lothian
Regiment), August 4th, 1914, to January
10th, 1915; Command Signalling Officer,
Scotland, till November 1st, 1916; in
India, January, 1917, to December, 1918;
appointed Cantonment Magistrate,
Murree, April 4th, 1917.

BUNTING, Sapper G. F. C. ... 1903-8   *f*
Hants (Fortress) Royal Engineers (T.).

BUNDOCK, Capt. C. S. 1882-5   *a*
Australian Remounts, in Egypt, 1915-16
(Disbanded); Australian Munition
Workers' Department, London, 1917 and
1918.

BURGESS, Pte. E. H. 1903-7   *a*
7th and 11th Bns., The Royal Fusiliers
(City of London Regiment); badly
wounded at Cambrai, October, 1918,
B.E.F.

†BURGESS, 2nd Lieut. P. G. ... 1903-8   *a*
The Queen's (Royal West Surrey)
Regiment, 8th (S.) Bn.; died, October
13th, 1915, a prisoner at Douai, of wounds
received at Loos, September 25th.

*Burt, Major A. E.   1906-11   *c*
The Oxfordshire and Buckinghamshire
Light Infantry, 8th (S.) Bn., Pioneers;
mentioned in despatches (twice); D.S.O.

*Burt-Smith, Capt. B. 1910-12   *a*
The London Regiment, 1/6th (City of
London) Bn. (Rifles); M.C. and Bar.

Butler, 2nd Lieut. A. H.   ... 1908-11   *a*
The Queen's Own (Royal West Kent
Regiment), 3/4th Bn. (T.).

†Campbell, 2nd Lieut. D. G.   ... 1901-4   *b*
A. Imp. F.; 1st Australian Division, 3rd
Infantry Brigade, 11th Bn.; served in
Gallipoli; killed at Mouquet Farm,
September 3rd, 1916.

†Capel-Cure, Capt. B. A.   ... 1907-10   *a*
The Gloucestershire Regiment, 2nd Bn.;
died of wounds, Bala-zir, Salonika,
October, 1916.

Capel-Cure, 2nd Lieut. L. H. ... 1903-8   *a*
The Prince of Wales's (North Staffordshire Regiment), 3rd Bn. (Reserve).

Cardew, 2nd Lieut. W. G.   ... 1898-1903   *a*
The Hampshire Regiment, 15th Bn.,
B.E.F., France.

†Card, 2nd Lieut. S. H.   ... 1899-1903
Prince Albert's (Somerset Light Infantry),
1st Bn.; slightly wounded, April 9th,
1917, and killed next day, near Fampoux,
in first battle of Arras.

*Carey, Bt. Lieut.-Col. A. B. ... 1887-9   *d*
Royal Engineers; R.M. Engineer Unit,
R.N. Division; C.M.G.; mentioned in
despatches (4 times); D.S.O.

23

CAREY, Capt. R. B. ... ... 1913-16 *d*
Royal Air Force.

CAREY, 2nd Lieut. C. O'D. ... 1901-8 *f*
Indian Army Reserve of Officers; 3/2nd
(Queen Victoria's Own) Rajput Light
Infantry (Allahabad); served with 2/10th
Jats till August 16th, 1918, (Jhausi).

CAREY, Major F. C. S. ... 1897-1901 *a*
Royal Army Ordnance Department.

CAREY, Lieut. G. M. ... ... { 1886-91 *f*
                               { 1897-*Master*
Unattached List (T.F.),Sherborne O.T.C.
(Physical Training).

CAREY, Major P. G. ... ... 1896-9 *f*
31st Punjabis; served in Mesopotamia.

*CAREY, Capt. R. O'D. ... ... 1905-10 *f*
The Duke of Wellington's (West Riding
Regiment), 2nd Bn.; taken prisoner;
returned, January, 1919; mentioned in
despatches (twice).

*CARR, Lieut. A. W. ... ... 1907-11 *a*
5th (Royal Irish) Lancers; mentioned in
despatches.

CARR, Lieut. P. G. ... ... 1911-14 *a*
7th (Princess Royal's) Dragoon Guards,
(serving with 4th Reserve Regiment of
Cavalry); invalided out, December, 1918.

†*CARR-ELLISON, a./Capt. O. F. C. 1909-14 *b*
The Northumberland Fusiliers, Special
Reserve Bn., from October, 1914, and,
later, 2nd Bn.; served in France, from
June, 1915; then with the Salonika Force
until July, 1918; returned to France and
was killed there, October 4th, 1918; Order
of the White Eagle (5th Class); mentioned in despatches.

CARR-ELLISON, C. F. C. 1915-18   *b*
Gentleman Cadet, Royal Military Academy, Woolwich.

CARRINGTON, 2nd Lieut. H. B.   ... 1901-6   *f*
Royal Army Service Corps (M.T.);
served in France.

†CARRINGTON, Capt. H. E.   ... 1899-1905   *f*
The Hampshire Regiment, 15th (S.) Bn.;
killed in France, at capture of Flers
(Somme), September 15th, 1916.

CARUS-WILSON, Capt. M. M.   ... 1908-13   *a*
The Dorsetshire Regiment, 1/4th Bn.(T.);
served in India and Mesopotamia from
December, 1914; on Staff as Record
Officer, at Basra.

†CARUTHERS-LITTLE, Capt.
A. W. P.   1899-1903   *b*
The Dorsetshire Regiment, 2nd Bn.;
Adjt. 5th (S.) Bn.; killed at the Dardanelles, August 7th or 8th, 1915.

*CARUTHERS-LITTLE, Major R. J. ... 1901-4   *b*
The Gloucestershire Regiment, 1/5th Bn.
(T.); served in France, Egypt and
Palestine; attached 1st Garrison Bn.
Northants Regiment; wounded; mentioned in despatches.

CATT, Lieut. N.   1908-12   *a*
R.F.A., 417th Battery; served with 42nd
Battery, in France.

CAUDWELL, 2nd Lieut. F. W. H.   1912-16   *f*
The Oxfordshire and Buckinghamshire
Light Infantry.

CHAFFEY, Capt. R. S. C.   ... 1885-9   *Price*
Territorial Force Reserve; Infantry.

*CHAFFEY, Col. R. A., V.D. ... 1868-73 *b*
Commanding Canterbury MilitaryDistrict
(No. 2); A.D.C. to Governor General,
1916; C.B.E.

*CHALKLEY, Capt. R. ... ... 1911-14 *d*
R.F.A., D/159th Brigade, 35th Division;
served in Gallipoli and France; mentioned
in despatches (twice); D.C.M.

CHANDLER, Capt. G. P. W. ... 1913-17 *f*
Royal Air Force.

*CHAPMAN, Capt. H. R. ... 1895-1900 *f*
Alexandra Princess of Wales's Own
Yorkshire Regiment, 5th Bn. (T.); men-
tioned in despatches.

†CHATTERIS, Capt. T. B. ... 1899-1900 *c*
The Sherwood Foresters (Nottingham
and Derbyshire Regiment), Special
Reserve; killed at Hooge, August 9th,
1915.

CHEATLE, Capt. C. T. ... ... 1894-8 *c*
R.A.M.C.; served in Egypt.

*CHESTER-MASTER, 2nd Lieut. A. G. 1903-9 *T.*
Armoured Car Division, (East Africa);
M.B.E.; mentioned in despatches.

*CHETHAM-STRODE, Capt. R. W. ... 1910-13 *b*
The Border Regiment, 3rd Bn. (Reserve),
attached 2nd Bn.; since April, 1918,
attached 18th Bn., Tank Corps; M.C.

*CHEVALLIER, Lieut. C. ... ... 1912-15 *f*
The Hampshire Regiment, 14th (S.) Bn.;
mentioned in despatches.

CHICHESTER, Lieut. O. ... ... 1888-92 *d*
The Devonshire Regiment, 6th Bn. (T.).

C

CHICHESTER, Pte. A. R.   ... 1893-6   *d*
The Royal Fusiliers (City of London
Regiment), 9th Bn.; wounded at Ypres,
July 31st, 1917.

†CHICHESTER, Capt. R. G. I.   ... 1887-91   *f*
The Highland Light Infantry, 2nd Bn. ;
killed near Zonnebecke, Belgium,
November 13th, 1914.

*CHURCH, Lieut.-Col. A. J. B.   ... 1880-6   *b*
Staff Paymaster, Army Pay Department ;
C.M.G. ; mentioned in despatches.

CHURCHILL, Lieut. W. F.   ... 1894-5   *c*
The London Regiment, 3/7th (City of
London) Bn.

CLAPIN, temp. Capt. A. C.   ... 1880-8   *T.*
Attached Special Service with the
' Service Sanitaire Militaire', Armée des
Vosges, November, 1914, till May, 1915;
Capt., O.C. No. 6 Company, Kent A.S.C.,
M.T. (T.).

†CLAPTON, 2nd Lieut. A. 1907-12   *f*
The Royal Fusiliers (City of London
Regiment), 32nd Bn. ; wounded and
missing in France, September 5th, 1916;
presumed killed.

†*CLARK, Capt. H. C.   1896-8   *a*
Royal Wiltshire (Prince of Wales's Own
Royal Regiment), B. Squadron ; died of
wounds received in action in France,
February 7th, 1918 ; M.C.

CLARK, Col. P. T.   1868-73   *c*
Late C.O. 1st Bn. Oxford Light Infantry,
(retired) ; Staff Captain for instructional
duties.

CLARKE, Lieut. A. B. ... .. 1908-10 *Prep.*
1914, H.M.S. Irresistible, which ship was
mined in Dardanelles ; served on H.M.S.
Inflexible, present at Battle of Jutland ;
finally, H.M. Destroyer, Lucifer.

CLARKE, Lieut. H. P. ... ... 1910-15 *b*
R.F.A.; attached 2/24th T.M.B., B.E.F.

CLARKE, Pte. M. N. ... ... 1912-13 *T.*
Inns of Court, O.T.C.

†CLARKE, Pte. W. W. E. M. ... 1911-13 *g*
The London Regiment, 1/4th (County of
London) Bn. (London Scottish) ; Des-
patch Carrier ; killed, July 1st, 1916.

†CLATWORTHY, 2nd Lieut. T. E. 1899-1901 *b*
Indian Army ; 37th Dogras ; killed in
Mesopotamia, January 6th, 1916.

COATH, Lieut. R. D. ... ... 1907-10 *a*
Scottish Horse, 2/2nd Bn.; attached Royal
Air Force.

COCHRANE, Lieut.-Col. G. L. ... 1887-91 *f*
The Durham Light Infantry, 3rd Bn.

COCHRANE, Lieut.-Col. J. E. C. J.,
D.S.O. ... ... 1884-6 *b*
R.F.A. (Reserve of Officers) Commanding
Ammunition Column, New Zealand
Artillery.

CODRINGTON, 2nd Lieut. K. de B. 1913-17 *c*
Indian Army ; 33rd Queen Victoria's
Own Light Cavalry.

COFFIN, Capt. A. S. ... ... 1900-4 *c*
Indian Army ; 28th Punjabis.

COLE, Pte. C. H. 1901-6   *a*
London Regiment; 2/28th Bn.

COLE, Rev. G. L. 1900-6   *a*
Army Chaplains' Department.

COLEBROOK, Capt. L. F. ... 1909-12   *a*
The King's Own (Royal Lancashire
Regiment), 8th (S.) Bn.; transferred
Administrative Captain, Royal Air Force,
April 18th, 1918.

*COLEMAN, Capt. G. D. 1907-11   *a*
The Norfolk Regiment, 3rd Bn.; mentioned War Services.

COLERIDGE, D. W. R. 1909   *b*
Public Schools' Bn. Royal Fusiliers and
Intelligence Staff; served in France.

COLLEY, 2nd Lieut. A. S. ... 1913-18   *g*
R.M.A.Woolwich and 72nd Battery, 38th
Brigade, Royal Field Artillery.

*COLLIER, 2nd Lieut. A. C. ... 1909-14   *b*
Royal Flying Corps, 3rd Squadron;
prisoner; mentioned for gallantry whilst
prisoner of war.

COLLIER, Lieut.-Col. W., M.D. ... 1871-4   *b*
Royal Army Medical Corps.

*COLLINS, 2nd Lieut. G. R. G. ... 1910-13   *a*
R.F.A., 33rd Divl. Artillery, 'A' Battery,
166th Brigade; mentioned in despatches.

COLLOT, Lieut. H. G. 1910-12   *a*
The Welsh Regiment, 3rd Bn.

†COLLOT, 2nd Lieut. T. A. ... 1908-12   *a*
Princess Charlotte of Wales's (Royal
Berkshire Regiment), 6th (S.) Bn.; killed
at the Battle of the Somme, July 1st, 1916.

COLMORE, Major H. ... ... 1896-1900 *f*
7th (Queen's Own) Hussars ; A.D.C.,
Personal Staff of Commander-in-Chief ;
attached 12th Lancers.

COMERFORD, Major R. H. J. ... 1876-9 *a*
(retired) 16th (County of London) Bn.
The London Regiment, Queen's (Westminster) Rifles, T.F.

COOKE, 2nd Lieut. F. H. ... 1902-5 *c*
R.N. Division.

COOPER, Pte. A. ... ... 1896-1900 *a*
The London Regiment, 1st Bn. London
Rifle Brigade ; resigned in October, 1914,
to take up duties in India.

COOPER, Lieut. A. H. ... ... 1903-7 *b*
Railway Transport Officer ; severely
wounded in France, November, 1915.

COOPER, Lieut. H. F. L. ... 1909-10 *d*
The Hampshire Regiment, 4th Bn. (T.).

COOTE, Capt. M. C. ... ... 1900-2 *c*
Indian Army ; 107th Pioneers.

CORFE, a./Sergt.-Major C. ... 1906-11 *a*
Canadian Engineers.

*CORNISH, Lieut. G. M. ... ... 1907-13 *a*
Grenadier Guards, 3rd Bn. ; M.C.

COSTLEY-WHITE, Capt.The Rev.H. 1901-3 *Master*
Liverpool College O.T.C.

COTTAM, Lieut. A. C. S. ... 1904-7 *a*
Royal Air Force ; Dental Officer ; No. 1
School Aerial Gunnery, Hythe and No. 8
Aircraft Acceptance Park, Lympne.

COTTER, Cadet H. ... ... 1914-18 *Prep.*
R.N.; Naval Cadet at Osborne.

COURTAULD, Capt. J. R. ... 1888-9   *d*
The Essex Regiment, 2/5th Bn. (T.).

COUSINS, Lieut. W. D. P. ... 1909-11   *a*
The Dorsetshire Regiment; enlisted in
Public Schools and University Corps,
1914; 2nd Lieut., 3rd Dorsets, May 20th,
1915; Lieut., July 1st, 1917; served with
1st Dorsets and 6th Dorsets in France,
with 2/4th Dorsets and I.A. in Egypt
and Palestine.

COWELL, 2nd Lieut. R. G. ... 1913-16   *g*
The Bedfordshire Regiment, 8th Bn.

Cox, 2nd Lieut. A. B. 1907-11   *c*
The Northamptonshire Regiment, 7th (S.)
Bn.

CRAVEN, Lieut. J. L. A. ... 1910-14   *c*
The Duke of Cornwall's Light Infantry,
3rd Bn. (Reserve).

CRAVEN, Lieut. N. F. de la B. 1898-1900   *b*
Royal Army Ordnance Department.

†CRAWHALL, Lieut. N. G. ... 1907-12   *a*
The Manchester Regiment, 1st Bn.; killed
July 7th, 1916, in Mametz Wood, France.

CRAWHALL-WILSON, 2nd Lieut. C.L. 1911-15   *c*
The Bedfordshire Regiment, 5th & 11th
Bns. (T.).

CRICHTON, Capt. E. C. 1903-7   *a*
Royal Army Medical Corps; attached
1/5th Bn. Suffolks, E.E.F.

31

†CRICHTON, 2nd Lieut. A. G. ... 1900-4   *a*

Enlisted in Seaforth Highlanders at Vancouver at outbreak of war; permitted to go to Dublin and enlist in ' D ' Co., 7th (S.) Bn. Royal Dublin Fusiliers; made Lance-corpl., December, 1914, Corpl., January, 1915, gazetted 2nd Lieut., R.D.F., April, 1915; missing, believed killed, 16th August, 1915, Suvla Bay.

†CROFT-SMITH, Lieut. E. S. ... 1906-9   *a*

The King's Royal Rifle Corps, 4th Bn.; missing, May 10th, 1915; assumed killed.

CRONSHAW, Lieut. T. J. 1904-9   *a*

Nigerian Field Force, B/3 Company.

†CROSBY, 2nd Lieut. A. B. L. ... 1910-13   *d*

The Durham Light Infantry, 5th Bn.; died of wounds in Arras, France, April 28th, 1917.

CROUCHER, Pte. A. A. 1914-16   *d*

Somerset Light Infantry, 3rd Bn.; and Hampshire Regiment, 2nd Bn.; served in France.

*CROWDY, Sergt. A. A. G. ... 1902-7   *a*

The Rifle Brigade (The Prince Consort's Own), 12th Bn.; formerly Lieutenant in Royal Army Service Corps, but invalided out, through ill-health, November 16th, 1917; D.C.M.

CROWTHER, Lieut. A. D. ... 1909-12   *b*

Royal Army Service Corps; served with Egyption Expeditionary Force; G.H.Q., May to June, 1916; Camel Corps, July, 1916, to August, 1917; R.A.S.C. (H.T.), August, 1917, to April, 1918; R.A.F., (scout pilot), April, 1918, to April, 1919.

CRUMP, Capt. G. H. ... ... 1912-13 *Master*
The Essex Regiment, 4th Bn. (T.).

*CUNNINGHAM, Bt. Major (a./Lieut.-Col.)
C.C. ... ... 1894-9 *j*
In Command, 2nd/107th Pioneers, Indian
Army; in 1914, Brigade-Major 1st Naval
Brigade; 1915, 12th Pioneers (The Khelat-
i-Ghilzie Regiment); G.S.O., 3rd Grade,
24th Division; 1917, in Command, The
Duke of Cambridge's Own (Middlesex
Regiment); wounded; mentioned in des-
patches; D.S.O.

*CUNNINGHAM, Major J. F., F.R.C.S. 1889-94 *f*
R.A.M.C.; Ophthalmic Specialist, B.E.F.;
O.B.E.

CURME, Lieut.-Col. D. E. ... 1887-9 *c*
R.A.M.C. /

†CUSTANCE, Surgeon G. W. M. 1896-1901 *c*
H.M.S. Hawke; drowned on H.M.S.
Hawke, October 14th, 1914.

*CUTHBERT, Capt. R. F. ... ... 1888-94 *a*
The Oxfordshire and Buckinghamshire
Light Infantry; 4th Bn. (T.); wounded
November 13th, 1917; M.C.

DALE, Lieut. C. B. M. ... ... 1908-12 *a*
The Northumberland Fusiliers, 2/4th Bn.
(T.); Royal Air Force, served in Mesopo-
tamia with 30th Squadron, afterwards in
Egypt.

*DAMMERS, Comdr. C. M. ... 1886-89 *Prep.*
R.N.; 1914, H.M.S. Ganges; 1917,
H.M.S. Europa, and H.M.S. Valkgrie,
mine sweeping in Eastern Mediterranean;
D.S.O., Chevalier of Légion of Honneur.

DAMMERS, Capt. E. H. F.   ... 1905-9   *a*
The Dorsetshire Regiment, 2/4th Bn.(T.).

*DAMMERS, Capt. (temp.Major) G. M. 1892-7   *a*
Dorset Yeomanry (Queen's Own), 1st Bn.
(T.F.) ; M.C., D.S.O.

DANDRIDGE, Capt. A. H.   ... 1902-4   *d*
Honourable Artillery Company, 'A'
Battery ; gassed at Doignies, France,
March 21st, 1918.

†DANDRIDGE, Lance-Corpl. A. P. 1902-1905   *d*
The King's Royal Rifle Corps, 20th Bn. ;
died of wounds in hospital at Abbeville
on August 6th, 1916.

†DANDRIDGE, Lieut. W. L.   ... 1908-12   *d*
R.A.M.C. ; died in hospital on October
5th, 1918, from wounds received in action
on October 3rd, 1918 ;   interred at
Haringhe, Belgium.

DANIEL, Lieut. A. H.   1902-6   *c*
Australian Imperial Expeditionary Force,
3rd Bn., 1st Infantry Brigade.

DAVIE, Cadet K. M.   1914-18   *b*
Household Brigade, Officer Cadet Bn.

*DAVIES, Lieut. E. H.   1906-7   *a*
1st Australian Contingent ; 3rd Field Company, Divisional Engineers ; transferred
to 15th Field Company, 1916 ;   served in
Egypt, Gallipoli and France ; M.C.

DAVIES, Capt. H. C. A.   ... 1910-14   *a*
The South Wales Borderers, 6th (S.) Bn.
(Pioneers).

*Davies, Major O. H.   ...   1898-1902   *f*
Royal Garrison Artillery ; 23rd Siege
Battery, B.E.F. ; M.C.

Davies, Lieut. W. W. N.   ... 1913-15   *a*
13th Hussars ; served in Mesopotamia.

Davis, Major E. 1903-*Master*
Unattached List (T.F.) ; Commanding
Sherborne School O.T.C.

*Davson, Major H. J. H.   ... 1895-8   *c*
Indian Army ; 82nd Punjabis ; served in
France, Mesopotamia and Palestine ;
D.S.O. ; mentioned in despatches, three
times.

Dawson, Capt. C. W. 1895-7   *c*
Royal Garrison Artillery.

Day, Capt. A. B. H.   1908-10   *a*
Royal Field Artillery, 215th Brigade ;
formerly in 1/2nd Hampshire Battery, 1st
Wessex Brigade, R.F.A. (T.) ; served in
India and Mesopotamia.

Day, Lieut. A. J.   1871-4   *a*
Late 2nd Lieut. Middlesex Yeomanry ;
assistant Recruiting Officer, 35th R.D.
Recruiting Area,Chichester ; Lieut.,¦434th
Agricultural Labour Corps ; Commandant,
Bognor Division, National Reserve.

Day, Lieut.-Col. C. R. L.   ... 1885-90   *c*
Commanding 2/5th Bn. (T.), The Hamp-
shire Regiment ; served in India, Decem-
ber, 1914 ;   on Staff, 9th Division,
Ootacamund, April-July, 1916 ; Egypt,
April, 1917 ; Palestine, till July, 1917 ;
transferred, from illness, T.F. Reserve,
November, 1917.

DAY, Lieut.-Col. D. A. L.   ... 1887-92   *c*

The Royal Warwickshire Regiment, 1st Bn. ; wounded at battle of Le Cateau ; prisoner of war, in hospital at Cambria, and at Hanover Hospital ; interned at Celle Schlosz, Halle, Augustabad and Heidelberg ; transferred to Holland, January 22nd, 1917 ; repatriated, November 16th, 1918.

*DEACON, Bt. Lieut.-Col. H. R. G.   1886-9   *b*

The Connaught Rangers, 1st Bn. ; attached Highland Light Infantry; D.S.O. and Bar, Légion d'Honneur, Chevalier ; mentioned in despatches (three times) ; served in Mesopotamia.

DE BURGH, 2nd Lieut. U.   ... 1913-18   *a*

Indian Army, Corps of Guides, 3rd Bn..

*DE COURCY-IRELAND, Capt. and Adjt. G. B.   1909-13   *a*

The King's Royal Rifle Corps, 16th Bn. (attached 5th Bn.) ; M.C., M.V.O., 1914-15 Mons Star.

DE COURCY-IRELAND, Lieut. L. K. 1911-14   *a*

The Devonshire Regiment, 11th (S.) Bn.; served in France with 1st Bn., May, 1916 ; wounded, July 24th, 1916, at Longueval (Somme) ; invalided out, Lieut. with Hon. rank, December 25th, 1917.

DENHAM, Lieut.-Col. L. S.   ... 1889-92   *f*

The King's (Liverpool Regiment) ; Capt. Reserve of Officers Middlesex Regiment ; commanding 19th (S.) Bn. (3rd City), The Duke of Cambridge's Own (Middlesex Regiment).

*Denis de Vitre, Lieut. E. C. ... 1911-15   *a*
Princess Charlotte of Wales's (Royal
Berkshire Regiment), 1st Bn.; men-
tioned in despatches.

de Pass, G. 1908-10   *f*
5th Highland Division Head Quarters,
T.F.; Staff car driver.

de Pass, Lieut. H. 1896-8   *c*
Royal Army Service Corps.

Derrick, Capt. L. 1909-11   *d*
Prince Albert's (Somerset Light Infantry),
1/4th Bn. (T.).

de Salis, 2nd Lieut. R. A. ... 1912-15   *a*
Indian Army, 3rd Skinners Horse.

de Steiger, Gunner, F. ... 1905-8   *d*
Royal Garrison Artillery; served in France
and Salonika with the 182nd S.A.S.A.C.
(Pack Mule Ammunition Column), and in
Palestine with the 379th Siege Battery.

de Winton, Major A. J. ... 1865-72   *a*
2nd Brecknockshire Bn. (T.), SouthWales
Borderers; O.C. 81st Labour Company,
B.E.F.

Dixey, Lieut. H. G. 1907-10   *f*
R.F.A.; N. Midland Brigade (T.).

Dixon, 2nd Lieut. M. D. ... 1913-18   *b*
Royal Engineers (Signal Depot).

*Dixon, Capt. W. A. 1905-7   *a*
The Duke of Edinburgh's (Wiltshire
Regiment), 3rd (S.) Bn.; attached (1918)
51st Graduated Bn., The Queen's (Royal
West Surrey) Regiment; wounded,
Salonika, April 24th, 1917; M.C.

*DIXON, Capt. and Adjt. G. S. ... 1908-13 *b*
Private in The Buffs (East Kent Regiment), 4th Bn. (T.), August 20th, 1914, to October 29th, 1914; 2nd Lieut. 2/4th Buffs (T.), October 29th, 1914, to June 6th, 1915; Lieut. and Adjt., June 6th, 1915, to August 31st, 1915; Capt. and Adjt., September 1st, 1915, to September 25th, 1917; on demobilization of 2/4th Buffs in September, 1917, attached to 1st (S.) Bn. Royal Guernsey Light Infantry, in France, September 26th, 1917; Assistant Brigade Major on 86th Brigade Staff, 29th Division, November 3rd, 1917, to February 14th, 1918; wounded at Armentières, Battle of the Lys, April 4th, 1918; returned as Adjt. to 1st (S.) Bn. Royal Guernsey Light Infantry, July 30th, 1918; O.B.E.; mentioned in despatches.

*DONNE, Col. H. R. B., C.B. ... 1873-8 *f*
G.S.O. 2nd Grade, War Office; C.M.G.; mentioned in despatches.

DOUGLAS, Rev. E. C. ... 1899-1904 *T.*
Army Chaplains' Dept., attached 15th Bn. K.O.Y.L.I.; B.E.F.

DOUGLAS, Pte. K. J. ... ... 1894-9 *T.*
Nigerian Land Contingent.

DOUGLAS, Comdr. S. C. ... ... 1895-6 *Prep.*
1914-16, in command of Submarines, and subsequently in command H.M.S. Alecto, Submarines Depot Ship; 1916, in command H.M.S. Q iii; 1917, joined staff of Admiral Sir Lewis Bailey, K.C.B.

DOW, Sergt. W. I. ... ... 1902-7 *b*
Honourable Artillery Company.

DRAKE, 2nd Lieut. W. B. ... 1886-90 *b*
The Devonshire Regiment; Garrison Bn.

DRAKE-CUTCLIFFE, 2nd Lieut.
B. H. H. ... ... 1913-15 *c*
The Devonshire Regiment; 1st Bn.

*DRESCHFELD, Lieut. S. E. ... 1911-16 *d*
Royal Air Force; Air Force Cross.

*DREWE, Capt. A. S. ... ... 1906-7 *b*
The Leicestershire Regiment (Reserve
of Officers), 3rd Bn. (Reserve); M.C.

DREWE, Rev. F. S., M.A., M.R.C.S.,
L.R.C.P. ... ... 1900-6 *b*
Medical Officer, Royal Air Force.

DRUITT, Capt. G. T. ... ... 1905-10 *T.*
The Hampshire Regiment, 7th Bn. (T.);
served in Egypt.

DRUITT, Capt. J. V. ... ... 1901-5 *T.*
The Hampshire Regiment, 7th Bn. (T);
served in Mesopotamia.

DRURY, Lieut. P. H. ... ... 1910-13 *a*
The South Wales Borderers, 1st Bn.;
attached R.A.F.

†DUCKWORTH, 2nd Lieut. W. H. ... 1910-14 *a*
The Lancashire Fusiliers, 20th (S.) Bn.;
died, April 14th, of wounds received in
France, March 23rd, 1916.

DUKE, Major A. B. C. ... ... 1902-6 *a*
R.F.A.; commanding 1093rd Battery,
Lahore, India.

DUKE, Capt. H. E. ... ... 1901-5 *a*
The Dorsetshire Regiment, 1/4th Bn. (T.)

DUMBLETON, Driver N. A. ... 1913-17   *T.*
Honourable Artillery Company.

DUNCAN, 2nd Lieut. D. C. ... 1901-2   *c*
The Royal Sussex Regiment, 3rd Bn.
(Reserve).

DUNCAN, 2nd Lieut. J. A. ... 1903-4   *c*
The Royal Scots Fusiliers, 9th (S.) Bn.

*DUNCOMBE-ANDERSON, Capt. W.... 1885-89   *a*
Reserve of Officers, 1904, Gazetted to
Cheshire Yeomanry, 1915 ; seconded for
duty as temp. Major, Labour Corps,
France, March,1917, to March,1919; twice
mentioned in despatches; Military O.B.E.

*DUNKIN, Major H., T.D. ... 1893-*Master*
Unattached List (T.F.) ; O.C. Commanding Sherborne O.T.C., till January 1st,
1918 ; mentioned for War Service.

*DUNNING, Capt. B. R. 1907-11   *f*
The Devonshire Regiment, 10th (S.) Bn. ;
mentioned in despatches.

DUNSTON, Lieut. A. E. A. ... 1909-14   *a*
The King's Own (Royal Lancaster Regt.),
1st Bn. (transferred from The Dorsetshire
Regiment, 2/4th Bn., T.) ; A.D.C.,1916;
Flying Officer, 30th Squad. R.F.C. (Mil.
Wing), 1916-1917 ; Political Dept., 1918.

DUSSEK, Capt. E. A. 1906-8   *d*
Royal Garrison Artillery.

†*DUVALL, Rev. (Capt.) J. R. ... 1902-6   *b*
Chaplain to 66th Brigade ; attached to
13th Manchesters, 12th Cheshires, 7th
Wilts ; served in France, 1915 ; in
Salonika, 1915-1917 ; died of wounds received in action, October 6th, 1917 ;
mentioned in despatches.

DYKE, Lieut.-Col. O. M. ... 1893-6 *a*
Indian Army; 21st Prince Albert Victor's
Own Cavalry (Frontier Force); Daly's
Horse.

†EAGAR, Lieut. D. G. ... ... 1912-17 *c*
Royal Field Artillery, B/160th Brigade;
killed in action, on edge of Wytschaete
Wood, September 28th, 1918.

†EAGAR, Lieut. F. R. ... ... 1907-12 *c*
Royal Field Artillery, 8th Division, 30th
Battery; killed at Fleurbaix, May 9th,
1915.

ECCLES, Lance-Corpl. R. E. A. ... 1911-14 *f*
Honourable Artillery Company, 1st
(Reserve) Bn.: discharged from Service,
November 2nd, 1918.

EDLIN, Lieut. P. A. M. ... 1911-14 *a*
The Royal Warwickshire Regiment, 2nd
Bn.; wounded, May 4th, 1917, and
October 13th, 1917.

†EDWARDS, Major B. ... ... 1897-9 *c*
Royal Garrison Artillery, Nigeria
Regiment, 123rd Siege Battery; killed in
France, March, 1917.

†*EGERTON, 2nd Lieut. B. R. ... 1911-14 *c*
Royal Engineers, 87th Field Company;
mentioned in despatches; killed at Lacelle,
France, October 23rd, 1918.

ELDERTON, Capt. M. B. ... 1907-*Master*
Royal Garrison Artillery; served in
France with 143rd Siege Battery, August,
1916, to June, 1917; and with 471st Siege
Battery, May, 1918, to November, 1918.

ELLERTON, Capt. W. M. ... 1882-3 *a*
H.M.S. Erin, (R.N.)

ELLIOTT, Rev. E. A. ... ... 1904-8 *a*
Y.M.C.A.; served with 4th Army, B.E.F.,
France.

†ELLIOT, 2nd Lieut. W. E. ... 1906-9 *a*
The Dorsetshire Regiment, 7th (S.) Bn.;
killed in France, September 26th, 1916.

†ELLIOTT, 2nd Lieut. E. ... 1912-14 *g*
Royal Field Artillery; died of wounds
received at Cambrai, October 8th, 1918.

†ELLIS, Major C. A. ... ... 1885-8 *Price*
The Cameronians (Scottish Rifles), 2nd
Bn.; killed in France at Neuve Chapelle,
March 10th, 1915.

ELLIS, Capt. G. R. ... 1899-1903 *a*
R.A.M.C.

†*ELSMIE, Lieut.-Col. G. E. D. ... 1880-2 *a*
Commanding 20th Deccan Horse; killed
in Mesopotamia; Officer Légion d'Honneur.

ELTON, temp. Capt. H. B. 1894-1901 *a*
Royal Army Medical Corps; attached
10th (S.) Bn., Devonshire Regiment;
served in France, September, 1915;
Salonika, November, 1915, to August,
1916; invalided out, November 21st, 1916.

*ENGLISH, Col. C. E. ... ... 1873-8 *a*
Royal Field Artillery; Reserve of Officers;
mentioned in despatches (twice); O.B.E.

*Ensor, Lieut.-Col. F. C. S. ... 1892-6   *a*
Army Ordnance Department ; in Royal
Garrison Artillery, Chief Ordnance Officer,
Mauritius, until November, 1915 ; Officer
i/c Ammunition, and later, Ordnance
Officer, Base Depôt, Alexandria, from
December 6th, 1915, to 1919 ; mentioned
in despatches and for 'services in
Mauritius'; Military O.B.E.

Evans, 2nd Lieut. D. C. R. J. ... 1913-17   *a*
Royal Garrison Artillery.

Evans, Midshipman R.   '... 1910-13 *Prep.*
R.N.; December, 1916, H.M.S. Royal
Sovereign.

Evan-Thomas, Lieut.-Col. A. ... 1858-62   *d*
7th Dragoon Guards.

*Everington, Major F. E. ... 1888-93   *f*
Royal Army Service Corps ; mentioned in
despatches.

Falconer, Major E. A. 1894-7   *a*
Royal Air Force.

*Farrer, Major E. R. B. ... 1905-10   *a*
Royal Army Service Corps (Special Re-
serve ; mentioned in despatches (twice) ;
M.C.

Fawcett, Lieut. C. H.... ... 1911-14   *d*
Royal Field Artillery, D/351 Battery;
served with the 73rd Battery, 5th Brigade, R.F.A., Lahore Division, in France
from September, 1916, to April, 1918;
gassed at Loos, April 9th, 1918.

†Fearnley-Whittingstall, Lieut.
G. H. 1907-9   *a*
(See 'Whittingstall').

*FENDALL, Col. (temp. Brig.-Gen.) C. P.,
    D.S.O. 1874-7   *a*
    Asst. Adjt. and Q.M.G., Administrative
    Staff, Dover Fortress; C.M.G., C.B.;
    mentioned in despatches (twice).

FENN, Col. E. H., C.I.E. ... 1861-5   *a*
    Late R.A.M.C., Worcester Territorial
    Force Association; employed under the
    War Office for several months; resigned
    owing to ill-health; died, November 24th,
    1916.

†FENN, Lieut. E. J. P. 1908-14   *a*
    The Royal Welsh Fusiliers; attached to
    1/5th Bn., The Essex Regiment; killed
    in action in Palestine, September 19th,
    1918.

FINCH, Lieut. W. 1887-91   *a*
    West Somerset Yeomanry (T.F.).

†FINDLAY, Capt. R. de C. ... 1883-7   *a*
    Seaforth Highlanders (Ross-shire Buffs,
    The Duke of Albany's), 4th Bn.; killed
    at Neuve Chapelle, 11th March, 1915.

FIRTH, 2nd Lieut. J. E. A. ... 1912-17   *f*
    Royal Garrison Artillery; 3rd (Reserve)
    Battery, R.H.A.

FISHER, Pte. H. W. T. ... 1911-13   *b*
    Honourable Artillery Company; served
    with 2nd Bn., in France, 1916; wounded
    and invalided home, January, 1917; in
    France, December, 1917, to June, 1918;
    then with 1st (Reserve) Bn.

*FISHER, 2nd Lieut. R. 1916-17   *f*
    R.N.V.R.; mentioned in despatches.

44

†FITCH, 2nd Lieut. D. ... ... 1911-13 *c*
Royal Field Artillery; served in France
and Flanders from August 20th, 1916,
until killed in the third battle of Ypres,
October 16th, 1917.

FLACK, 2nd Lieut. H. L. ... 1906-9 *c*
Royal Army Service Corps.

FLOWER, Lieut. E. J. ... ... 1910-14 *a*
R.F.A.; served in France; 1914-15 Star.

FLOWER, 2nd Lieut. W. M. ... 1911-14 *a*
5th Reserve Cavalry Regiment.

*FOLEY, Major W. B. ... ... 1903-7 *a*
R.A.M.C.; served in France; with
Salonika Force from December, 1915, to
November, 1918; with 28th C.C.S. during
whole period; Surgical Specialist to unit
from October, 1918; mentioned in despatches (twice); O.B.E.

†FOLLIOTT, 2nd Lieut. J. ... ... 1912-16 *c*
Durham Light Infantry; killed in France,
September 19th, 1918.

FOOT, Lieut. H. J. ... ... 1903-7 *T.*
The Welsh Regiment, 1/4th Bn. (T.);
served in the Dardanelles with 53rd Divi-
sion; severely wounded at Suvla Bay
Landing, August 10th, 1915; subsequently
Asst. Staff Officer at Headquarters; Pem-
broke Dock Garrison; then War Dept.
Land Agent to the Western Command,
Chester.

*FORD, Surgeon-Gen. R. W., D.S.O. 1874-5 *d*
Deputy Director of Medical Services in
Egypt; K.C.M.G., C.B.

†FORREST, Lieut. E. A. A. ... 1904-10   *a*
The Gloucestershire Regiment, 11th (S.)
Bn.; died of blood-poisoning at Malta,
December 9th, 1915.

FORREST, Bombardier L. B. L. ... 1906-10   *a*
Australian Force; 5th Divisional Ammunition Column ; served in France.

*FORSHAW, Capt. H. P. 1892-4   *a*
The King's Own (Royal Lancaster Regiment), 2/5th Bn. (T.) ; M.C.

FOSTER, 2nd Lieut. E. L. P. ... 1912-16   *a*
Indian Army, 39th Garhwal Rifles.

FOSTER, Capt. T. B. G. ... 1899-1903   *f*
The Cameronians (Scottish Rifles),1st Bn.

Fox, 2nd Lieut. E. L. W. ... 1912-6   *b*
Indian Army, 39th Garhwal Rifles.

Fox, 2nd Lieut. R. de V. R. ... 1912-16   *g*
Indian Army, 45th Sikhs.

*FRASER, Major A. J. 1888-9   *b*
Royal ArmyService Corps; Supply Depôts
Northampton and Le Havre,August,1914,
to 1917 ; Assistant to D.A.D. of Supplies,
H.Q., 2nd Army, France, April to Novem-
ber, 1917 ; Assistant to A.D. of Supplies,
G.H.Q.,Italy, November, 1917, to March,
1919 ; mentioned in despatches, Decem-
ber, 1917, and May, 1918 ; D.S.O. and
La Croie al Merite di Guerra.

FRASER, Sergt. G. D. 1908-11   *b*
Canadian Expeditionary Force.

†FRASER, 2nd Lieut. V. A. D. ... 1914-17   *b*
Indian Army, 3rd (Q.V.O.) Corps of
Guides ; killed, November, 1919, in Ex-
pedition on N.W. Frontier.

*FREEMAN, Major C. T. 1908-11   *b*
Royal Air Force; D.S.O., A.F.C.

FREEMAN, 2nd Lieut. P. B.   ... 1916-20 *Master*
Worcester Regt.; and Sherborne O.T.C.

FRENCH, Surgeon Lieut.-Comdr. A.
G. V.   1896-1901   *a*
H.M.S. Vindex; 1914, was on H.M.S.
Carnarvon in Falkland Islands action;
1917, was on H.M.S. Marshal Ney (Dover
Patrol) in action with enemy destroyers;
1918, on H.M.S. Vindex in Eastern
Mediterranean (anti-submarine work).

†FREUND, Corpl. E. W. T.   ... 1909-14   *b*
Royal Engineers, 186th Company; died
of wounds near Merville, December 22nd,
1915.

*FREWEN, Lieut.-Col. L.   ... 1903-6   *f*
The King's Royal Rifle Corps, 8th (S.)
Bn.; served in France, May, 1915 to
January, 1917; invalided, May, 1917;
mentioned in despatches (twice); D.S.O.

*FRINK, Capt. F. C. B. 1881-6   *b*
The South Staffordshire Regiment, 10th
(S.) Bn.; attached Labour Corps; men-
tioned in despatches.

FRINK, 2nd Lieut. H. R. C.   ... 1913-17   *b*
4th (Royal Irish) Dragoon Guards.

FRISBY, Lieut. N.   1909-13   *b*
The Duke of Edinburgh's (Wiltshire
Regiment), 7th (S.) Bn.

†FROST, 2nd Lieut. A. C.   ... 1911-14   *d*
Princess Louise's (Argyll and Sutherland-
shire Highlanders), 11th (S.) Bn.; killed
in France, September 27th, 1915.

FROST, 2nd Lieut. B. D.   ... 1911-15   *b*
Essex Regiment; attached Royal Air
Force,

†FROST, Lieut. J. J.   1910-14   *d*
The Northumberland Fusiliers, 11th (S.)
Bn.; Senior Machine Gun Officer;
killed in France, July 7th, 1916.

FUTCHER, 2nd Lieut. G. H. C.   ... 1905-7   *c*
The Sherwood Foresters (Nottingham-
shire and Derbyshire Regiment), 10th
Bn.; from 1915 to 1917 a trooper in 1st
King Edward's Horse, (The King's
Oversea Dominions Regiment).

*GALLOWAY, Major (temp. Lieut.-Col.)
A. G.   1892-4   *a*
Royal Army Service Corps; mentioned
in despatches; D.S.O.

GARDNER-SMITH, Rev. P.   ... 1902   *d*
Served in France with Church Army.

GARNIER, Lance-Corpl. The Rev.
G. R.   1894-99   *a*
Enlisted in 1915 in M.T., A.S.C., saw
service in France from August, 1916, to
January, 1918, when discharged unfit.

GARSTIN, temp. Capt. C. F.   ... 1894-7   *T.*
Chinese Labour Corps, 23rd Company.

GARSTIN, Major W. A. M.   ... 1895-9   *T.*
Government of India Political Department.

*GATER, Major C. E. H. 1901-5   *a*
R.A.M.C.; Special Reserve; mentioned
in despatches.

*GEE, Lieut.-Col. F. W., M.B.   ... 1876-80   *d*
Indian Medical Service, attached to 5th
Cavalry; mentioned in despatches (thrice);
C.I.E.

GEIPEL, 2nd Lieut. L. H. H.   ... 1905-7   *a*
Royal Field Artillery ; 4th Northumbrian
(Company of Durham) (Howitzer) Am-
munition Column (T.).

†GERRARD, Capt. P. N. 1884-7   *d*
Malay States Volunteer Rifles; killed
in the Singapore mutiny while Commandant, Prisoner of War Camp, Singapore, 1915.

GIBBONS, 2nd Lieut. H.   ... 1912-15   *g*
Royal Military College, Sandhurst ; 1st
Bn. The Devonshire Regiment (attached
3rd Bn.).

†GIBBONS, 2nd Lieut. J.   ... 1912-16   *g*
The Dorsetshire Regiment, 6th Bn.;
died of wounds at Etaples, June 6th, 1917.

GIBBS, 2nd Lieut. A. R.   ... 1899-1904   *a*
The Worcestershire Regiment, 7th Bn.;
served in France ; attached 13th Norfolks.

GIBBS, 2nd Lieut. C. B.   ... 1905-9   *c*
The Duke of Edinburgh's (Wiltshire
Regiment), 6th (S.) Bn.

GIBSON, Assist. Paymaster C. de V. 1906-9   *b*
H.M.S. ' Arrogant.'

*GIBSON, Capt. E. R. 1906-9   *d*
Royal Field Artillery ;   Staff Captain,
R.A., 3rd Corps, B.E.F.; M.C.; men-
tioned in despatches (twice).

*GIBSON FLEMING, Capt. and Bt.-Major
H. 1901-4   c
The Highland Light Infantry, 9th
(Glasgow Highland) Bn. (T.) ; Assistant
Director, Ministry of Munitions ; men-
tioned in despatches.

GILBERT, Capt. R. F. E. ... 1885-7 *Price*
The Norfolk Regiment, 4th Bn. (T.).

GILL, Lieut.-Col. J. W. 1868-73   a
Royal Army Medical Corps.

*GLASGOW, Bt. Lieut.-Col. (Hon. Brig.
General) W. J. 1874-7   c
The Queen's (Royal West Surrey) Regiment ; O.C. 7th Bn. in France ; 50th
Infantry Brigade and Tank Corps Training Centre (1917-18) ; mentioned in
despatches ; C.M.G.

GODFREY, 2nd Lieut. D. S. ... 1907-10   b
The Dorsetshire Regiment, 3rd Bn.
(Reserve) ; attached 8th Bn., Devonshire
Regiment.

†GOLDSMITH, Lieut. H. M. ... 1899-1904   a
The Devonshire Regiment, 3rd Bn. ;
Machine Gun Officer, 25th Brigade ;
killed near Fromelles, May 9th, 1915.

GOODRICK, Gunner G. C. C. ... 1906-8   a
Royal Field Artillery, 187th Brigade.

GOODWYN, Cadet J. N. 1913-17   b
Household Brigade, Officer Cadet Bn.

50

GOODWYN, Capt. N. P. ... 1898-1900 *b*
The Worcestershire Regiment, 7th Bn.;
relinquished commission on account of ill
health, caused by wounds, with the
honorary rank of Captain, February
14th, 1917.

*GORDON, Capt. C. A. ... 1897-1902 *T.*
Indian Army; 11th Rajputs (Duke of
Connaught's Own); A.D.C., H.Q., 12th
Brigade, I.E.F. 'D'; served in Mesopo-
tamia; mentioned in despatches; M.C.,
D.S.O.

GORDON, Major G. S. ... ... 1893-8 *b*
Indian Army; 35th Scinde Horse.

GOSLING, Sergt. H. ... ... 1906-9 *a*
Honourable Artillery Company, 'B'
Battery.

GOSSLING, 2nd Lieut. A. C. ... 1914-17 *c*
Royal Field Artillery.

GOULD, 2nd Lieut. G. ... ... 1914-17 *a*
Royal Air Force; served in France with
41st Kite Balloon Section, R.A.F.

*GOVER, Capt. A. C. ... ... 1898-1901 *a*
Indian Army, 121st Pioneers; M.C.

GRACE, Sub. Lieut. E. ... ... 1908-10 *Prep.*
1916, H.M.S. Australia.

GRAHAM, Paymaster Sub. Lieut.
G. D. M. ... ... 1910-12 *d*
R.N.R., H.M.S. King George V.

51

GRAHAM-MONTGOMERY, Capt. G.
J. E. ... ... 1908-11 *b*
The Hampshire Regiment, 12th (S.) Bn.

GRANGER-BROWNE, 2nd Lieut. H.F. 1913-16 *b*
The Devonshire Regiment, 16th Bn.

*GRANVILLE, Major C. (temp.
Lieut.-Col.) ... ... 1886-9 *b*
The Devonshire Regiment, 3rd Bn.,
attached 1st Bn.; O.B.E.; mentioned in
despatches.

*GRAVES, Capt. B. ... ... 1902-3 *a*
Served as Medical Officer to 5th and 6th
Bns., The Prince of Wales's (North
Staffordshire Regiment) and to 10th and
13th Bns., The Royal Fusiliers (City of
London Regiment), in France, and to 19th
Brigade, Royal Field Artillery, in
Salonika; Opthalmic Surgeon in charge
of 56th and 82nd Army Opthalmic
Centres from Armistice till demobilization;
M.C.

†GRAY, 2nd Lieut. G. E. M. ... 1908-12 *f*
The Northumberland Fusiliers, 14th (S.)
Bn.; killed, July 14th, 1916, at Bazentin
le petit.

†GRAY, Capt. H. M. ... ... 1908-10 *f*
The Royal Fusiliers (City of London
Regiment), 11th Bn.; severely wounded
in attack on Thiepval, 1916; wounded
and missing (since assumed killed), August
10th, 1917, in Ypres—Menin Road battle.

GREATHEAD, Lieut. A. M. ... 1901-1904 *c*
Royal Engineers, 56th Field Company.

*GREATHEAD, a./Major J. M. ... 1901-3 *c*
Royal Engineers; mentioned in despatches ; M.C.

GREENHILL, Capt. H. M. ... 1898-1900 *b*
The Dorsetshire Regiment, 3rd Bn. (Reserve).

GREENSLADE, Lieut. R. S. ... 1909-11 *d*
Somerset Royal Horse Artillery ; Motor Machine Gun Service; 100th Squadron, R.A.F.; served in France; prisoner of War in Germany for 14 months.

*GREENSTREET, Bt. Lieut.-Col. C. B. L. ... ... 1885-8 *a*
Royal Engineers; mentioned in despatches (four times, for work in Mesopotamia); Serbian Order of the White Eagle, 4th Class with Swords.

*GREGORIE, Bt. Lieut.-Col. H. G. 1893-7 *a*
The Royal Irish Regiment, 2nd Bn.; mentioned in despatches (thrice); Légion d' Honneur, Croix d' Officier ; D.S.O.

GREGORY, 2nd Lieut. C. A. ... 1912-16 *c*
The Essex Regiment.

*GREVILLE, Capt. a./Lieut.-Col. G. G. F. F. ... ... 1899-1901 *a*
The Prince of Wales's Leinster Regiment (Royal Canadians), 1st Bn.; mentioned in despatches.

GREVILLE-HARSTON, Brig.-Gen. C. 1860-4 *T.*
Chief Inspector of Arms and Ammunition, Canadian Expeditionary Forces Headquarters Staffs; served in France.

†GRIERSON, Lieut. S. D. 1912-17   *f*
Seaforth Highlanders (Ross-shire Buffs,
The Duke of Albany's); killed in France,
August 30th, 1918.

*GRIFFIN, Major (a./Lieut.-Col.)
J. A. A. 1905-8   *a*
The Lincolnshire Regiment, 2nd Bn.;
April and May, 1918, a./Lieut.-Col., com-
manding 2nd Bn., Princess Charlotte of
Wales's (Royal Berkshire Regiment);
mentioned in despatches (twice) ; D.S.O.

GRIMLEY, 2nd Lieut. A. T. ... 1912-16   *c*
The Dorsetshire Regiment, 3rd Bn.

GROVE, Lieut. G. 1902-6   *f*
King's African Rifles; temp. A.D.C. to
Lord Buxton.

†GROVE, 2nd Lieut. (a./Capt. and Adjt.)
P. C. 1911-15   *f*
Seaforth Highlanders (Ross-shire Buffs,
The Duke of Albany's), 2nd Bn.; killed at
the battle of Arras, April 11th, 1917.

†GROVES, Corpl. J. S. 1908-10   *a*
30th British Columbia Horse, attached
3rd Canadian Signal Corps as a Motor
Despatch Rider; died near Hazebrouck,
France, January 17th, after an accident on
the night of January 15th, 1916, whilst
carrying a message.

†GROVES, Lance-Corpl. R. E. ... 1910-11   *a*
11th Canadian Mounted Rifles; killed in
action, March 27th, 1917.

GUIMARAENS, Paul ... ... 1910-14 *Prep.*
R.N.; 1917, H.M.S. Alsatian (10th Cruiser
Squadron).

*GULLICK, Capt. C. D. 1906-11   *d*
The Buffs (East Kent Regiment), 6th (S.)
Bn.; M.C. and bar.

†GUNNING, Lieut. J. W. 1911-14   *g*
The Duke of Edinburgh's (Wiltshire Regi-
ment), 1st Bn.; killed at the battle of
Bapaume, March 21st, 1918.

GUPPY, 2nd Lieut. R. 1907-8   *b*
The Dorsetshire Regt, 3rd Bn. (Reserve).

*GURNEY, Capt. J. C. 1906-12   *f*
The Northamptonshire Regiment, 7th (S.)
Bn.; G.S.O., 3rd Grade, 2nd Army Head-
quarters; mentioned in despatches (twice);
Belgian Croix de Guerre; O.B.E.

GWYTHER, Major E. J. 1888-91   *T.*
Leicester Regiment, attached 273rd Infantry Bn.; gassed in Mametz Wood.

†GWYTHER, Corpl. P. H. 1892-3   *a*
South Staffordshire Regiment; killed at
Ypres, January 12th, 1917.

*HAES, a./Capt. C. P. M. ... 1890-3   *u*
Royal Army Service Corps; served in
France; Officer Order de L'Etoïle Noire.

*HALL, Major (temp.Lieut.-Col.) E.G. 1897-9   *d*

117th Mahrattas ; D.A. Q.-M.-G., Headquarters Staff, Simla ; served in the 6th
(Poona) Division, Mesopotamia ; wounded
at Zaim, November 17th, 1914, and at
Ctesiphon, November 22nd, 1915; mentioned in despatches (thrice) ; Order of
Kara George,4th Class,with swords; C.I.E.

†HALLIDAY, 2nd Lieut. C. G. R. ... 1911-14   *g*

Royal Engineers ; entered Woolwich,
December, 1914; transferred to Chatham,
July, 1915 ; went to France, February,
1916, to 1st Field Squadron, R.E.,attached
to 1st Cavalry Division; was transferred to
225th Field Co., R.E., on June 1st, 1917.
Killed at Ypres on June 13th, 1917.

HALLIDAY, Lieut. G. R. 1909-10   *b*

Royal Garrison Artillery ; No. 1 Battery ;
No. 3 Siege (Reserve) Brigade ; served in
India, January, 1915, to January, 1917,
with 1st Wessex Brigade, R.F.A. (T.),
and then in Mesopotamia with 74th Brigade, Heavy Artillery, until December,
1918.

HAMILTON, Lieut. C. F. H.   ... 1911-16   *d*

Royal Field Artillery ; served in France
from January 3rd, 1917, till wounded on
March 25th, 1918.

HAMLING, Lieut. H. H. 1902-4   *c*

King's African Rifles, 3rd Bn. ; served 15
months as private in 2nd Rhodesian
Regiment.

HAMMOND, W. C. W. ... ... 1911-12 *g*
American Protective League (Secret Service), also British Recruiting Mission, Chicago.

HAMMOND, Major W. P. ... 1897-1900 *a*
Indian Army, 18th Infantry.

HAMPTON, Capt. R. W. ... ... 1904-8 *f*
The Royal Fusiliers (City of London Regiment), 8th (S.) Bn.; attached 5th Bn.; on Staff, Embarkation, Tilbury Docks.

†HAMPTON, Rifleman W. ... ... 1905-9 *f*
The London Regiment; joined 1st Bn. London Rifle Brigade, in August, 1914; went to France, November 7th, 1914; shot in the neck by a sniper, January 16th, 1915, whilst wiring, and died May 14th, 1915, at a nursing home in London.

HANKEY, Major C. A. A. ... 1882-6 *a*
The Highland Light Infantry,14th(S.)Bn.; Assistant Provost Marshal, Winchester.

*HANKEY, Major (temp. Col.) S. R. A. 1888-92 *a*
(Ret.), South Irish Horse (late 3rd Dragoon Guards), Dep. Director of Remounts, 3rd Army, B.E.F.; Special Reserve; South Irish Horse; mentioned in despatches; D.S.O.

HARDY, Capt. H. de L. ... ... 1908-12 *c*
Indian Police, and Indian Army Reserve of Officers; died at Denapur, after a short illness, on August 30th, 1919.

HARE, Lieut. P. V. 1913-15   *c*
The Artists Rifles; 8th Bn. Sherwood
Foresters ; 7th Bn. Gloucester Regiment;
and 270th Company Machine Gun Corps.

HARRIS, Pte. J. B. 1899-1904   *b*
Canadian Infantry, 188th Bn.;   and
Canadian Flying Corps.

*HARRIS, 2nd Lieut. M. W. S. ... 1911-14   *g*
The Duke of Cambridge's Own (Middlesex
Regiment), 4th Bn.; M.C.

HARRIS, Cadet R. L. A.... ... 1913-18   *f*
R.E. Cadet School.

HARRIS, Midshipman R. R. ... 1914-15   *g*
H.M.S. Iron Duke.

HARRIS, Capt.W. J., M.D., F.R.C.P, 1880-4   *f*
R.A.M.C.(T.F.); Neurologist,3rd London
General Hospital.

HARRISON, Lieut.-Col. H. ... 1883-9   *a*
Indian Political Department.

HARSTON, 2nd Lieut. W. W. ...1913-17   *a*
The Dorsetshire Regiment, 3rd Bn.

HART, Pte. G. 1915-17   *b*
Inns of Court O.T.C.; 3rd Bn. London
Scottish; 51st Bn. Gordon Highlanders;
served in France.

HARVEY, Lieut. C. D. W. ... 1908-11   *T.*
The Dorsetshire Regiment, 7th (S.) Bn.;
later attached to 1/6thGurkhas,Abbotabad;
wounded on the Somme, 1916, and at
Cambrai, June, 1918.

HARVEY, Lieut. R. W. 1912-13   *T.*
The Dorsetshire Regiment, 3rd Bn. (Reserve); attached 6th Bn. in France; also to Royal Air Force (Observer), 42nd Squadron.

HASLER, Lieut. F. G. 1912-15   *g*
Royal Field Artillery; served in France, October, 1917, to February, 1918, with C/177th Brigade, R.F.A., 16th (Irish) Division; invalided out, 1919.

*HATTON-HALL, Capt. H. C. ... 1907-9   *c*
The King's Own Scottish Borderers; attached to Machine Gun Corps and subsequently to Tank Corps; M.C.

*HAWKEY-SHEPHERD, Major J. G. 1899-1902   *f*
County of London Yeomanry, 2nd Coy. (Westminster Dragoons),T.F.; mentioned in despatches; M.C.

HAWKINS, 2nd Lieut. C. L. M. ... 1913-17   *a*
Dorsetshire Regiment, 3rd Bn.; served previously in Inns of Court O.T.C. and 20th Officer Cadet Bn.

*HAWLEY-EDWARDS, Lieut. S. F. 1895-1900   *a*
Mentioned in despatches.

†*HAY, Capt. G. W. 1893-6   *a*
The Loyal North Lancashire Regiment, 3rd Bn. (Reserve); August, 1914, placed on Coast defence at Felixtowe; December, 1914, joined 1st Bn. L. N. Lancs. in France; December 21st, 1914, slightly wounded at Festubert; May 9th, 1915, killed in action at Richebourg l'Avonée; mentioned in despatches.

*HAY, Mr. K. R.   1887-91   *a*

Civilian M.O., 1st London General Hospital ; rejected for general service; O.B.E.

HAYNES, Pte. S. H. `   1901-5   *d*

The London Regiment, 28th (County of London) Bn. (Artists' Rifles) (T.F,) ; invalided out.

HAYTER, 2nd Lieut. E. G. E.   ... 1908-10   *a*

Royal Field Artillery, 68th Brigade, 17th Division ; served in Egypt : with 11th Division, in Gallipoli, 1915 ; with 10th Division in 1st Serbian campaign, 1915-16; in France, 1917; gassed and invalided home ; in Palestine, 1918.

HAYTER, Lieut. F. C. E.   ... 1914-16   *a*

Royal Air Force, 16th Squadron ; served in France, June, 1918 ; worked for 18th Corps and then for 8th.

HAYTER, Lieut. G. R. E.   ... 1910-13   *a*

Royal Air Force, 12th Squadron ; served in France ; previously in the Hampshire Regiment, 9th (Cyclist) Bn. (T.).

HAYTER, 2nd Lieut. T. J.   ... 1901-3   *a*

The Loyal North Lancashire Regiment, 7th (S.) Bn.; attached 6th (S.) Bn. (38th Brigade, 13th Division); served in Gallipoli till evacuation, November, 1915 ; discharged owing to ill-health.

*HEMPSON, Capt. G. O. 1903-7   *a*

R.A.M.C. ; served in France and Cyprus ; mentioned in despatches.

HEMPSON, 2nd Lieut. V. A. ... 1900-4 *a*
Royal Field Artillery; badly gassed in
France, 1917.

*HENDERSON, Lieut. E. C. ... 1902-5 *b*
The Northumberland Fusiliers, 6th Bn. ;
attached 21st Bn. ; severely wounded at
Greenland Hill, Arras,June 5th,1917; M.C.

*HENNIKER-GOTLEY, Major G. R. ... 1908-11 *c*
The Prince of Wales's (North Staffordshire Regt.); 91st Coy.,Machine Gun Corps;
mentioned in despatches (thrice) ; D.S.O.

*HENRI, Major P. R. ... ... 1905-9 *c*
The Royal Fusiliers (City of London Regi-
ment), 1/3rd Bn. ; D.S.O. ; M.C, and bar ;
Croix de Guerre.

HERBAGE, Lieut. K. A. ... ... 1912-13 *c*
Royal Field Artillery; served in France and
with the North Russia Relief Force; gassed.

†HERBAGE, Pte. S. H. W. ... 1910-13 *c*
The London Regiment, 1st Bn., London
Rifle Brigade; went to France, November
4th, 1914, and was killed in action, January
20th, 1915.

*HERBERT, Major D. M. A. ... 1910-14 *c*
Indian Army ; 82nd Punjabis ; served in
Mesopotamia ; mentioned in despatches ;
M.C.

HERIZ-SMITH, 2nd Lieut. The Rev.
E. E, A. ... ... 1912-17 *Master*
Unattached List(T.F.); Sherborne O.T.C.

*HESSE, Major J. H. B. ...   ... 1886-90 *Price*

Royal Army Service Corps ; Mechanical
Transport ; served in France ; mentioned
in despatches.

*HEXT, 2nd Lieut. A. C. 1908-12   *a*

2nd East Riding of Yorkshire Yeomanry
(T.F.) ; M.B.E.

HEXT, Lieut.-Col. F. M.   ... 1875-8   *a*

The Devonshire Regiment, 10th (S.) Bn. ;
served in France, 1915 ; Macedonia, 1916 ;
gazetted commandThe Sherwood Foresters
(Nottinghamshire and Derbyshire Regt.),
July 25th, 1916 (at Home) ; employed
under War Office (M.I. 8 branch), 1917
and 1918.

*HEXT, Capt. (temp. Major) G. T. B. 1894-8   *c*

Indian Army ; served in British East
Africa ; D.S.O.

*HEYWOOD, Lieut.-Col. Sir G.P., Bart. 1893-7   *a*

Yeomanry, Territorial Force ; Staffordshire (Queen's Own Royal Regt.) ; served
with the Egyptian Expeditionary Force,
1915-18 ; mentioned in despatches; D.S.O.

†HICKS, Col. F. R.   1882-9   *a*

The Hampshire Regiment ; August 22nd,
1914, went to France, 2nd in Command
of 1st Bn., and was wounded at LeCateau.
November, 1914, returned to France in
Command of 1st Bn.; May 8th, 1915, again
wounded, at La Brique, near Ypres, and
died at Guy's Hospital on June 12th, 1915.

HINDLE, 2nd Lieut. M. D.   ... 1914-17

Indian Army ; 2/35th Sikhs.

*HITCH, Lieut.-Col. A. T.　　... 1907-11　　*b*
The Lincolnshire Regiment; a./Lieut.-Col.
in command 8th (S.) Bn.; served with 6th
(S.)Bn.,and 3rd(Reserve)Bn.,The Bedfordshire Regt.; 2nd in command 11th(S.) Bn.,
The Royal Warwickshire Regt.,November
and December, 1917; wounded, February
12th,1916; mentioned in despatches; D.S.O.

HITCHCOCK, Capt. R. V.　　... 1898-1902　　*f*
Royal Engineers.

HITCHINGS, Lieut N. J. ...　　... 1884-7　　*d*
East African Transport Corps.

HOBSON, Capt. E. R. C.　　... 1910-13　　*a*
British West Indies Regiment; attached
Z Squadron, Royal Air Force.

HODDER, Bt. Col. W. M.　　... 1874-7　　*c*
Royal Engineers (Reserve of Officers).

*HODGES, Capt. A. P. ...　　... 1910-12　　*c*
Royal Field Artillery; 2nd Lieut., July
17th, 1914; France and Belgium, 1914-
1918; Siberia, 1919; promoted Lieut.
June 9th, 1915; a./Capt., August 25th,
1916; a./Major, September 25th, 1916;
Capt.,November 3rd,1917; Military Cross,
January 1st, 1918; severely wounded,
March 21st,1918; mentioned in despatches,
January 1st, 1919.

†HODGES, 2nd Lieut. H. B.　　... 1910-14　　*b*
The King's Own (Yorkshire Light In-
fantry), 2nd Bn.; August, 1914, entered
Sandhurst; December 23rd, 1914, gazetted
2nd Lieut.; March, 1915, went to France;
April 18th,1915,killed at Hill 60,near Ypres.

*HODGES, Capt. J. F. 1902-6   *a*
Princess Victoria's (Royal Irish Fusiliers),
2nd Bn.; mentioned in despatches ; M.C.
and bar.

HODGSON, 2nd Lieut. E. 1918-*Master*
Unattached List (T.F.); Sherborne School
O.T.C.

†HODGSON, Lieut. R. E. 1908-13   *a*
The King's (Liverpool Regiment), 4th
Bn.; attached R.A.F.; Pilot, July, 1918 ;
killed in Belgium, while flying over the
German trenches, September, 15th, 1918.

*HODSDON, Major J. W. B., M.D.,
F.R.C.S. 1872-5   *b*
R.A.M.C. (T.F.) ; 2nd Scottish General
Hospital; O.B.E. (Military) ; mentioned
for War Services.

HOGG, Capt. A. R. 1910-14   *a*
The Queen's Own (Royal West Kent
Regiment), 7th (S.) Bn.; served in France,
December 8th, 1915, till October 26th,
1917; then wounded (second time) and
had foot amputated.

HOLDEN, Lieut. (temp. Capt.) E. G. 1909-14   *a*
Princess Charlotte of Wales's (Royal Berk-
shire Regiment); attached 139th Bn.,
Machine Gun Corps.

*HOLDEN, Capt. G. H. R., M.A., M.D., B.C.
(Cantab.), M.R.C.S. (Eng.), L.R.C.P.
(London) 1877-82   *a*
R.A.M.C. (T.F.) ; 3rd General Hospital,
Oxford ; seconded for Service at Reading
War Hospital, March, 1915, Officer in
Charge of Officers' Section ; mentioned for
War Services.

HOLDEN, a./Corpl. R. W. ... 1914-18   *a*
Inns of Court O.T.C. and 2nd Bn., King's
Royal Rifle Corps.

†HOLMES, 2nd Lieut. B. R. G. ... 1908-12   *b*
Royal Field Artillery, 3/4th Northum-
brian (Co. of Durham) (Howitzer) Brigade
(T.) ; Commissioned, July, 1915 ; joined
London Anti Aircraft defences, and was in
charge of a Station ; killed in action, in
France, October 1st, 1917.

HOLMES, Lieut. B. S. (see Scott-Holmes)

*HOLMES, Major P. L. 1903-7   *b*
R.N.A.S.; D.S.C.; mentioned in despatches.

HOLT, Lieut. G. F. 1882-6   *b*
Royal Army Medical Corps.

HOMFRAY, Lieut. H. C. R. ... 1905-8   *f*
2nd Glamorgan Yeomanry (T.F.); retired
on account of ill-health, March 1st, 1917.

HOMFRAY, Pte. K. 1910-12   *a*
Royal Army Service Corps (M.T.); served
with Mesopotamian Expeditionary Force.

HOMFRAY, Capt. R. 1905-10   *a*
The Worcestershire Regiment, 1/7th Bn.;
served with Italian Expeditionary Force.

HONNYWILL, Capt. G. W. ... 1889-95   *a*
Royal Army Service Corps.

*HOOPER, Capt. A. W. 1904-8   *a*
Royal Garrison Artillery, Forth R.G.A.
(T.); 152nd Siege Battery ; M.C.

65

HOOPER, Lieut. C. J. ... ... 1911-14 *d*
The Dorsetshire Regiment, 4th (Reserve)
Bn.; served in France.

*HOOPER, Capt. D. S. ... ... 1902-6 *a*
The Dorsetshire Regiment, 3rd (Reserve)
Bn.; The Tank Corps; wounded, July,
1916; mentioned in despatches; M.C.

†HOOPER, 2nd Lieut. L. J. ... 1908-13 *a*
The Dorsetshire Regiment, 7th (S.) Bn.,
attached 5th Bn.; served in Gallipoli;
killed on September 26th, 1916, near
Mouquet Farm, on the Somme.

HOOPER, Corpl. M. ... ... 1906-10 *d*
Dorset Yeomanry (Queen's Own), 1st Bn.;
served in Egypt; wounded.

HOPE, Major L. C. ... ... 1886-9 *f*
The Dorsetshire Regiment, 2nd Bn.

HOPE, Sergt. P. P. ... ... 1905-6 *T.*
Royal Engineers, Motor Cycle Despatch
Rider.

HORNE, Lieut. G. S. ... ... 1902-5 *f*
The Royal Fusiliers (City of London
Regiment), 3/4th Bn.

*HORNIDGE, Capt. E. S. ... ... 1901-6 *c*
Royal Army Service Corps; mentioned in
despatches; O.B.E.

HORNIDGE, 2nd Lieut. M. S. ... 1913-16 *c*
North Irish Horse.

HORSFALL, Lieut. T. M. ... 1897-1902 *a*
Royal Army Service Corps (H.T.), late
Border Regt.; served in France, Salonika,
Bulgaria, Constantinople, Turkey in Asia,
The Caucasus; invalided home from
Russia, in 1919.

HORTON, Sub-Lieut. A. ... ... 1911-13 *Prep.*
Royal Navy; 1917, H.M.S. Agincourt;
1918, H.M.S. Orion.

†HOSKINS, 2nd Lieut. F. D. ... 1910-14 *d*
The Prince of Wales's (North Staffordshire Regt.),1st Bn.; August, 1914, entered
Sandhurst; December 10th,1914, gazetted
2nd Lieut., N. Staffs. Regt.; March,1915,
went to France to 1st Bn. at Ypres; July,
1915, appointed Bn. M.G. Officer; October 2nd, 1915, died from Shell Splinter
wound in the head received previous day.

HOSKINS, Lieut. N. M. ... ... 1908-11 *d*
Enlisted in The London Regiment, 1/14th
(County of London) Bn.(London Scottish),
attached to 3/14th Bn. Commissioned to
Balloon Section, R.A.F.

*HOVIL, Major R. ... ... 1894-6 *d*
Royal Field Artillery, 'A' Battery, 75th
Brigade; served in France, with Guards'
Division; mentioned in despatches; D.S.O.

How, Lieut.-Col. A. P. ... ... 1881-5 *a*
Indian Army, 114th Mahrattas; 2nd in
Command.

How, Capt. D. ... ... 1888-92 *a*
The Welsh Regiment, 20th (S.) Bn. (3rd
Rhondda) (late 3rd Bn., Reserve).

HOWARD-SMITH, Cadet J. ... 1914-18   *c*
Royal Field Artillery; 212th Battery, 2
B. Brigade.

HOWELL, 2nd Lieut. H. L. ... 1913-17   *d*
Royal Garrison Artillery.

HOWSE, 2nd Lieut. E. C. ... 1914-18   *d*
Loyal North Lancashire Regiment,1stBn.;
previously R.M. College, Sandhurst.

*HUDSON, Capt. (temp. Lieut.-Col.) and
Bt. Major C. E. 1905-10   *c*
The Sherwood Foresters(Nottinghamshire
and Derbyshire Regiment), 2nd Bn.; mentioned in despatches (5 times); V.C.;
D.S.O.; M.C.; Croix de Guerre; Italian
silver medal for valour.

HUDSON, Capt. T. H. 1903-6   *c*
The Sherwood Foresters(Nottinghamshire
and Derbyshire Regt.), 2/4th Bn. (extra
Reserve), attached 2nd Bn.

HUGHES, Lieut. H. C. 1907-11   *b*
Royal Field Artillery, 2/3rd Hampsnire
Battery, 1st Wessex Brigade (T.); served
in India, January 7th, 1915, to September
16th, 1916; then in Mesopotamia, with
56th Brigade, R.F.A.,until December 31st,
1917;and in France until wounded, August
26th,1918; demobilized,January 27th,1919.

*HULBERT, Major T. E. 1895-7   *f*
Indian Army, 3rd Skinner's Horse; served
in France, November, 1914, to August,
1916; attached to 10th Lancers in Mesopotamia, November, 1916, to July, 1917;
appointed Commandant, Branch School of
Musketry, Satara, October, 1917; mentioned in despatches.

*HUNNYBUN, Major K. ... ... 1901-6 *f*
The Huntingdonshire Cyclist Battalion ;
attached 7th Bn., Prince Albert's(Somerset
Light Infantry ; mentioned in despatches ;
D.S.O.

HUNT, Lieut. E. G. ... ... 1895-99 *a*
(late Capt., unattached List, T.F.) ; Royal
Welsh Fusiliers, 3rd (Reserve) Garrison
Bn. ;   September, 1917, Gas Officer,
attached R.A.M.C. Depôt, Blackpool.

HUNT, 2nd Lieut. W. H. ... 1912-16 *g*
Royal Garrison Artillery.

HUNTER, Capt. P. D. ... ... 1887-92 *c*
Royal Army Medical Corps ; Neurologist,
Gateshead War Hospital.

†HYLAND, 2nd Lieut. H. B. ,.. 1910-11 *c*
Enlisted in East Kent Yeomanry, Septem-
ber,1914 ; transferred to 20th (S.) Bn. (3rd
Rhondda),TheWelsh Regiment,in Spring,
1915, and was Commissioned there in
Autumn, 1915 ; transferred to 100th Coy.,
Machine Gun Corps ; went to France,
March, 1916 ; killed in action at High
Wood,Battle of the Somme,18th July,1916.

ILLINGWORTH, Sub-Lieut. H. A. ... 1913-17 *a*
R.N.V.R.

*IREMONGER, Col. E. A. ... ... 1878-81 *f*
(late Durham Light Infantry); The Depôt,
The Queen's Own (Royal West Kent
Regt.); mentioned forWarServices; G.B.E.

IREMONGER, Lieut.-Col. R. G. ... 1869-72 *f*
(Ret. Indian Army), Staff-Capt., G.S.O.,
3rd Grade.

JACKMAN, Sub-Lieut. W. F.   ... 1909-11   *c*
R.N.R., H.M.S. Goshawk.

†JACKSON-TAYLOR, 2nd Lieut. J. C.   1912-16   *c*
The King's Shropshire Light Infantry,
1st Bn. (Commissioned from Sandhurst) ;
killed at Cambrai,France,March 21st,1918.

JACKSON-TAYLOR, Major P. S.   ... 1909-14   *c*
The Herefordshire Regiment, 1st Bn. ;
obtained Commission in 1914 ; went to
Gallipoli,1915, and was there till wounded,
November, 1915 ; joined Royal Flying
Corps, January, 1916, and went to France
in summer of 1917, rising to be Major
(now Capt., R.F.C., Regular Army).

*JACOB, Lieut.-Col. A. L., C.I.E.   ... 1886-9   *a*
Indian Army (Political Department) ;
O.B.E.

*JACOB, Brig.-Gen. A. le G., C.I.E.,
     D.S.O.   1877-84   *a*
Commandant 106th Hazara Pioneers ;
G.S.O., 1/4th (Quetta Division); A.A.
D. Q.M.G., Base Headquarters, Mesopo-
tamia Expeditionary Force ; A.D.C. to
H.M. the King ; mentioned in despatches ;
C.M.G.

*JACOB, Lieut.-Gen. Sir C. W.   ... 1875-81   *a*
G.O.C.,2nd Army Corps,B.E.F.,from May
28th, 1916 ; previously commanded Dehra
Dun Brigade, January to September, 1915;
Meerut Division to November, 1915 ; 21st
Division to May, 1916 ; mentioned in
despatches (nine times) ; C.B. ; K.C.B. ;
K.C.M.G.; C.M.G.; Commandant Légion
d'Honneur ; Croix de Guerre ; Grand
Officier, Ordre de la Couronne ; Grand

Officier, Order de Leopold avec Croix de
Guerre (Belgian); Grand Officier, Légion
d'Honneur (French); Distinguished Con-
duct Medal (America).

*JAMES, Bt. Lieut.-Col. A. H. C. ... 1887-90 *Price*
The South Staffordshire Regiment, 1st
Bn.; Asst. Provost Marshal, 3rd Corps,
August, 1914, to October, 1915; then
Provost Marshal, 3rd Army, to August
4th, 1918; then Provost Marshal Forces
in Great Britain, with rank of temp. Brig.-
Gen.; wounded, October, 1914; mentioned
in despatches (four times); Officier de la
Légion d'Honneur; M.V.O.; D.S.O.

JAMES, 2nd Lieut. C. J. B. (formerly
Scholey) ... ... 1912-17 *a*
London Regiment, 12th (County of Lon-
don) Bn. (The Rangers).

JAMES, C. N. ... ... 1901-5 *a*
Indian Police; District Superintendant of
Police, 4th Grade.

†JANASZ, 2nd Lieut. J. G. G. ... 1907-12 *b*
The Dorsetshire Regiment; gazetted to
3rd Bn. (Reserve), November 4th, 1914;
sent to France and attached 2nd Bn.,Wilt-
shire Regt., in March, 1915; killed, near
Festubert, June 15th, 1915.

JEFFERSON, Asst. Paymaster E.A.R. 1910-14 *f*
Served on H.M.H.S. Mauretania,and H.M.
Transports, Andania, Carpathia and Czar-
itza ; attached to Naval Transport Service
(Mercantile Marine).

JEFFREYS, 2nd Lieut. R. H. ... 1910-11 *c*
The Welsh Regiment, 20th (S.) Bn. (3rd
Rhondda); resigned, 1917, on account of
ill-health.

†JEFFREYS, Lieut. W. S. 1911-14   *c*
The Welsh Regiment, 13th (S.) Bn. (2nd
Rhondda); served in France, 1915-16;
reported wounded and missing, in Mametz
Wood, July 9th, 1916; later reported killed.

†JENKINS, Lieut. R. B. 1910-14   *b*
The South Wales Borderers; gazetted to
5th (S.) Bn., September 19th, 1914; entered Sandhurst, December 31st, 1914;
gazetted to 2nd Bn., S. W. Borderers,
attached R.F.C., on June 16th, 1915;
gazetted Flying Officer, September, 1915;
joined No. 9 Squadron, in France, December 19th, 1915; died of wounds in France,
January 17th, 1916, received in fight with
a Fokker plane.

JENKINSON, Lance-Sergt. E. A. ... 1907-8   *d*
The Royal Fusiliers (City of London Regiment), 28th Bn. (Reserve).

JENNINGS, Lieut. G. W. 1901-4   *a*
Royal Field Artillery; attached G.H.Q.,
the Forces in Great Britain, June, 1917,
to August, 1918; temp. Secretary, British
Embassy, Madrid, September, 1918, to
April, 1919.

*JEPHSON, Lieut. J. H. 1911-14   *a*
Royal Garrison Artillery, 2/No. 2 Com-
pany, Lewes, Sussex; and 24th Squadron
R.A.F.; mentioned for War Services.

†*JESSON, Major R. W. F.   ... 1901-5   *d*
The Duke of Edinburgh's (Wiltshire Regiment); joined as 2nd Lieut., 5th (S.) Bn.,
in August, 1914; wounded in Gallipoli;
mentioned in despatches; killed, while 2nd
in Command of Regt., near Kut, February
22nd, 1917.

*JOHNSON, Lieut.-Col. W. R. ... 1902-5   *a*
   The Essex Regiment, 1/7th Bn. (T.); mentioned in despatches (twice); D.S.O.;C.B.E.

*JOHNSTON, Bt. Major D. S. ... 1900-4   *a*
   Royal Engineers; mentioned in despatches.

JOHNSTONE, Lieut. C. A. ... 1901-3   *a*
   The Dorsetshire Regiment, 6th Bn.; served
in France; Liaison Officer with Portugese
Corps; joined 3rd Bn., Rifle Brigade.

JOHNSTONE, Lieut. C. R. ... 1894-7   *d*
   The Dorsetshire Regiment, 7th (S.) Bn.;
Transport Officer.

JOHNSTONE, Capt. M. B. S. ... 1906-9   *f*
   Army Remount Service; served in
Salonika; commanding 49th Remount
Squadron, 1918.

*JONES, Capt. H. E. 1894-7   *a*
   Royal Sussex Regiment, 13th (S.) Bn.;
gazetted 2nd Lieut., September, 1915;
served in France from March, 1916, to
October, 1918; a./Capt. and a./Staff-Capt.,
116th Infantry Brigade; wounded, September, 1918; on the Wytschaete Ridge;
mentioned in despatches (twice); M.C.

JONES-EVANS, Sub-Lieut. E. J. L. 1913-15   *c*
   R.N.V.R.; served on H.M.S. Lookout
and H.M.S. Porpoise.

JUDKINS, 2nd Lieut. B. E. H. ... 1898-1901   *a*
   13th Hussars (serving with 12th Reserve
Regiment of Cavalry).

*KEIR, Surgeon Comdr. W. W. ... 1891-3   *a*
Royal Navy; mentioned in despatches;
C.M.G.; Légion d'Honneur (Chevalier).

KELLY, Capt. B. J. R. 1906-10   *a*
The South Wales Borderers, 3rd Bn.
(Reserve).

*KEMP, Major F. W. 1893-9   *a*
New Zealand Medical Corps; D.A.D.M.S.,
N.Z. Division (October, 1918); M.C.

KENDLE, Major F. C. 1890   *Price*
Royal Marine Artillery; Instructor of
Gunnery, Eastney Barracks, Portsmouth;
served on H.M.S. Agincourt, August 8th,
1914, to July 25th, 1915.

KENDLE, Capt. G. H. 1900-2   *c*
Royal Marine Artillery; H.M.S. Monarch.

†*KENDLE, Major R. H. 1890   *Price*
The Suffolk Regiment, 5th Bn. (T.); as
Hon. Capt. in Regulars, volunteered for
foreign service; 1915, gazetted Major,
made a district Musketry Instructor, and
received Volunteer Decoration; went to
Gallipoli, July, 1915; killed in a bayonet
charge at Sulva Bay, August 12th, 1915.

†*KESTELL-CORNISH, Capt. R. V. ... 1908-14   *a*
Gazetted The Dorsetshire Regt., 1st Bn.,
August, 1914; Adjutant, November, 1916;
joined Staff, as G.S.O.3, September 3rd,
1917; mentioned in despatches (thrice);
M.C. and bar; twice wounded, the second
time at Houlthulst Forest on March 8th,
1918,from which he died on June 17th,1918.

E

†KIDNER, Corpl. F. E. ... ... 1901-6 *b*

The London Regiment ; came home from Russia and joined 16th Bn. (Queen's Westminster Rifles); landed in France, January 26th, 1915 ; died, February 20th, 1916,of wounds received near Armentières, February 19th.

*KIDNER, Major W. E. ... 1897-1901 *b*

Royal Engineers ; 2nd Queen Victoria's Own Sappers and Miners ; 33rd Divl. Signal Coy., Lahore Division ; I.E.F.. January, 1915, to October, 1915 ; trained 40th Divl. Signal Coy., and took it to France, June 1st, 1916 ; recalled to India, October, 1917 ; General Staff ; M.C.

†KING, 2nd Lieut. E. W. ... 1893-9 *a*

Royal Field Artillery ; came over from F.M.S. to join up, in August, 1917 ; went to France, April, 1918 ; wounded, October 19th, 1918, and died next day.

*KINGSTONE, Capt. J. J. ... ... 1906-11 *a*

2nd Dragoon Guards (Queen's Bays) ; Staff-Capt., 1st Cavalry Brigade ; served in France from August 14th, 1914, to 1919; mentioned in despatches (twice) ; M.C.; D.S.O.

KIRKWOOD, Pte. J. T. ... ... 1893-6 *f*

Royal Air Force ; served in France with observation balloons.

KIRTON, Lieut. K. S. ... ... 1910-12 *d*

Royal Army Service Corps ; attached to 47th Brigade, Royal Garrison Artillery, in France ; formerly in West Somerset Yeomanry, 1st Bn. ; served in Gallipoli.

†KITSON, 2nd Lieut. E. G. T. ... 1909-15   *c*
The Duke of Cornwall's Light Infantry;
gazetted to 3rd Bn. (Reserve),August 14th,
1915 ; went to France, March, 1916, and
joined 6th Entrenching Bn.; attached 1st
Bn.,June,1916; died, September 3rd,1916,
from wounds received the same day, at
Guillemont, in the Battle of the Somme.

KNIGHT, Corpl. J. E. 1903-4   *a*
Royal Field Artillery.

*KNOBEL, Capt. H. E. 1885-90   *a*
Staff-Capt., 2nd Canadian Infantry Brigade; gassed atYpres ; invalided out,April,
1917; mentioned in despatches (twice),

KNÖS, Capt. J. E. 1910-13   *d*
2nd Worcestershire (Queen's Own
Worcestershire Hussars) ; wounded at
Beersheba, November 8th, 1917.

*KNOX, Major J. H. 1899-1905   *f*
Honourable ArtilleryCompany,'A'Battery;
attached to Royal Garrison Artillery ;
wounded ; M.C.

KRAUSE, Lieut. E. H. 1905-11   *d*
The Durham Light Infantry, 10th Bn.

KRAUSE, Pte. R. A. 1912-16   *d*
The Royal Fusiliers (City of London Regiment), 5th Bn.

*LACEY, Major C. D. 1897-1900   *a*
The King's Royal Rifle Corps, 9th (S.)
Bn.; mentioned in despatches(thrice); M.C.

†LACEY, 2nd Lieut. E. S. 1901-5   *a*
The Duke of Cambridge's Own (Middlesex
Regiment), 16th (S.) Bn.(Public Schools),
as Private, in September, 1914; commissioned to 11th Bn.,Cheshire Regiment;
missing since October 21st, 1916, presumed killed.

LAMB, Major D. G.   1886-8   *b*
The Rifle Brigade (The Prince Consort's
Own); 2nd in Command, 14th (S.) Bn.;
served in France, with 1st Bn.; commanded a composite battalion in 4th Division; invalided home in 1917; 2nd in
Command,Reserve Bn.,The Rifle Brigade.

*LAMBERT, Lieut.-Col. W. J.   ... 1887-92   *a*
The King's (Liverpool Regt.); Commanding 14th (S.) Bn. (temp.); 29th Lancers
(Deccan Horse), Indian Army; mentioned
in despatches; D.S.O. and two bars.

LANE, Gunner D. H.   1912-16   *f*
Royal Field Artillery, 'A' Battery, 6th
Reserve Brigade.

†LARGE, Capt. H. E.   1894-7   *d*
The Rifle Brigade (The Prince Consort's
Own), 10th (S.) Bn.; died, October 9th,
1915, of wounds received that day, near
Laventie, France.

†LARNDER, Lieut. E. M. 1907-12   *f*
West India Regiment; with 1st Bn. at
Sierra Leone at out-break of war. After
trying all other means of getting to the front,
he resigned his Commission in September,
1916, came to England, and enlisted in the
6th Dorsets in October, 1916; went to
France in December, 1916; killed in action
in front of Arras, April 23rd, 1917 (rank,
Private).

*Laurie, Major H. 1888-93   *a*
Supt., Remount Squadrons; O.B.E.; mentioned for War Services.

*Law, Capt. R. W. R. 1896-7   *b*
The King's Royal Rifle Corps (60th Rifles); Staff-Capt., Headquarters, Southern District, Cork, Ireland; O.B.E.; M.C.

*Leckie, Lieut.-Col. V. C. ... 1898-1902   *f*
Royal Army Veterinary Corps; Commanding No. 15 Veterinary Hospital, Rouen; mentioned in despatches; D.S.O.

Lee, 2nd Lieut. C. J. 1914-16   *d*
The Devonshire Regiment, 1st Bn.

Leeds, 2nd Lieut. H. J. ... 1905-8   *a*
Royal Field Artillery.

†Leeds, 2nd Lieut J. S. 1901-5   *a*
Honourable Artillery Company, Infantry; came from Argentine to join the H.A.C., September, 1914; given Commission in H.A.C., December, 1914; went to France, July, 1915; killed in the Crater at Hooge, September 19th, 1915.

*Leeds, Bt. Lieut-Col. T. L. ... 1883-6   *a*
Indian Army, 59th Scinde Rifles (Frontier Force); served in Mesopotamia; mentioned in despatches (thrice); C.M.G.; D.S.O.

*Lee-Warner, Rev. A. 1893-7   *a*
Chaplain to Forces (T.), 1916; Senior C.F. (T.), 1918; Attached Cheshire Regiment, 1st Bn.; mentioned in despatches.

78

*LEE-WARNER, Lieut.-Col. H. G. 1896-1900   *a*
  Royal Field Artillery, 41st Brigade; mentioned in despatches (twice); D.S.O.; M.C.

LEE-WARNER, 2nd Lieut. J. ... 1903-8   *a*
  The Northumberland Fusiliers, 2nd Garrison Bn.

*LEGGE, F. C. 1886-92   *a*
  Indian Defence Force; East Indian Railway, 1/37th Bn.; Deputy Coal Controller, Calcutta; C.B.E.

†LEGGE, Capt. R. G. 1892-6   *a*
  The Devonshire Regiment, 2nd Bn.; killed in France, December 18th, 1914.

*LE HUQUET, Capt. and Bt. Major R. 1901-5   *d*
  The Bedfordshire Regiment, 3rd Bn.; in Command of 8th Bn. from June, 1917, to February, 1918, when disbanded; wounded, May 13th, 1918, when in command 6th Bn., Northamptonshire Regiment; mentioned in despatches.

†LEIGH, 2nd Lieut. H. G. T. ... 1899-1902   *a*
  Labour Corps, France; previously served in German S.W. Africa with 8th African Artillery; also in Artillery Cadet School, Leckfield; died in France, November 11th, 1919, from pneumonia.

*LEIGH, Capt. (a./Major) H. V., M.B., B.S., M.R.C.S., L.R.C.P. 1900-4   *a*
  R.A.M.C.; Registrar, successively, of Nos. 31, 27 and 71, General Hospitals; from August, 1917, Officer in Charge, Medical Division, No. 71, General Hospital; mentioned in despatches.

LEONARD, 2nd Lieut. R. F. W. ... 1914-18   *a*
Royal Field Artillery.

LESLIE, Col. P. N.   ...   ... 1882-5 *Price*
Indian Army.

LETHBRIDGE, 2nd Lieut. A. B. ... 1893-4   *a*
Interpreter.

LETHBRIDGE, Lieut. J. C. B. ... 1901-11   *b*
Royal 1st Devon Yeomanry (T.F.); served
in Egypt and France from January 1st,
1916, to March, 1919.

*LEWIS, Capt. (Bt. Major, acting Lt.-Col.)
F. E. C. 1908-12   *a*
The East Lancashire Regiment; attached
47th Machine Gun Battalion ; mentioned
in despatches (twice).

LEWIS, Pte. H. E. C. 1912-13   *c*
The Prince of Wales's (North Staffordshire Regiment), 6th Bn.

*LEY, Capt. C. E. A. 1902-6   *c*
Joined the Canadian Contingent, 1914 ;
joined R.E. at home, 1915, and went with
Egyptian Expeditionary Force to Palestine same year ; gained M.C. at taking of
Jerusalem ; placed in charge of Telegraphs
in Aleppo district.

*LEY, Lieut.-Col. E. M. 1898-1902   *a*
The King's Royal Rifle Corps, 3rd Bn. ;
mentioned in despatches ; D.S.O.

LEY, Capt. R. H. 1895-8   *a*
Canadian Expeditionary Force ; '88th
Victoria Fusiliers ; joined Balloon Section
in Palestine Campaign.

LEYBORNE-POPHAM, Capt. and Adjt.
F. H. A. 1905-8   *d*
The Bedfordshire Regiment, 6th (S.) Bn.

†*LIMBERY, Capt. C. R. 1905-8   *d*
The South Staffordshire Regiment,1st Bn.;
went to France with 1st B.E.F., August,
1914, and was twice wounded at Loos, and
again in May, 1916; mentioned in despatches; M.C.; killed at Mametz, July
1st, 1916.

†*LIMBERY, Capt. K. T. 1905-10   *d*
R.A.M.C.; went to France as a dresser,
September 4th, 1914; to Russia with an
Ambulance, October, 1915; to France
again, March, 1916; mentioned in despatches; M.C.; killed in action, September
26th, 1917.

*LINDLEY, Lieut. (a./Capt.) W. M.   1905-7   *d*
Royal Engineers (T.F.); Officer Commanding 8th Corps Heavy Artillery,
Signals; served in France continuously
from November 6th, 1914; mentioned in
despatches; M.C.

LLEWELLIN, Lieut. E. C.   ... 1908-12   *d*
The Monmouthshire Regiment, 1/1st Bn.;
wounded at St. Julian, April 25th, 1915.

†LLEWELLIN, 2nd Lieut. W. M. J.   1913-16   *a*
The South Wales Borderers, 1st Bn.;
went from School to Sandhurst, January,
1917; gazetted 2nd Lieut.,December,1917;
went to France, April, 1918; wounded,
June, 1918; killed, on patrol at Cambrai,
August 17th, 1918.

†LLOYD, 2nd Lieut. G. L. B. ... 1912-14 *Master*
The Dorsetshire Regiment, 5th (S.) Bn. ;
killed, August 6th, 1915, in the landing at
Suvla Bay, Gallipoli.

LOCKWOOD, 2nd Lieut. D. D. ... 1912-16 *b*
Royal Air Force.

LONSDALE, Capt. P. ... ... 1886-90 *d*
East Lancashire Regiment (Reserve of
Officers) ; 1st Class District Officer, N.
Provinces, Nigeria.

LOTT, 2nd Lieut. D. B. ... ... 1914-18 *f*
12th Officer Cadet Bn. ; attached 3rd Bn.,
The Bedfordshire Regiment.

†*LOTT, Lieut. J. C. ... ... 1908-13 *f*
The Royal Fusiliers (City of London Regi-
ment), 18th (S.) 1st Public Schools' Bn.
(Special Reserve of Officers), and The
East Lancashire Regt., 3rd Bn., attached
11th Bn. ; wounded, March, 1917, and
March, 1918 ; killed in action in France,
April 13th, 1918 ; M.C.

*LOTT, Lieut. R. C. ... ... 1906-11 *f*
The Lancashire Fusiliers, 12th (S.) Bn. ;
wounded (in Macedonia), September, 1916;
mentioned in despatches ; attached General
Staff, War Office, August, 1917 ; mentioned for War Services.

*LOVEBAND, Col. F. R. ... ... 1877-82 *a*
West India Regiment (Bt.-Col.) (Reserve
of Officers) ; The Prince of Wales's Own
(West Yorkshire Regiment) ; Command-
ing 1st Garrison Bn. ; mentioned for War
Services.

Low, Rev. P. W. 1896-1901   *b*
52nd Brigade (Infantry), 17th Division
(Army Chaplains' Department).

Lowis, Lieut.-Col. F. C., C.I.E. ... 1886-91   *d*
Royal Engineers ; served in Persia.

†*Luard, Lieut.-Col. E. B. ... 1884   *c*
The King's Shropshire Light Infantry, 1st
Bn. ; mentioned in despatches (thrice);
D.S.O. ; mortally wounded, April 21st,
1916, at the re-taking of the Ypres Lange-
mark Trenches ; died, April 24th, 1916.

Luard, Lieut.-Col. G. D. ... 1880-3   *c*
The Cameronians (Scottish Rifles).

Lucas, Lieut. D. 1901-6   *a*
Honourable Artillery Company; mentioned for War Services.

Luff, Lieut. C. M. C. 1912-14   *a*
Royal Army Service Corps.

*Lumley, Capt. D. O. 1909-13   *d*
The Duke of Edinburgh's (Wiltshire Regiment), 5th (S.) Bn. ; served in Gallipoli ;
wounded, July 23rd, 1915 ; Deputy Assistant Inspector of Recruiting, Southern
Command, April 25th, 1916, to September
13th, 1917 ; then employed at War Office ;
transferred to General List for duty with
Ministry of National Service ; Head of
Registration Branch, August 1st, 1918;
O.B.E.

Lund, Capt. R. J. S. 1910-13   *a*
Princess Charlotte of Wales's (Royal Berk-
shire Regiment), 1/4th Bn. (T.) ; 60th
Squadron, Royal Air Force.

*LUNT, Rev. G. C. L. ... 1899-1905 *a*
Temporary Chaplain to the Forces, B.E.F.
(1917); M.C.

*LUSH, Rev. J. A. ... ... 1898-1900 *c*
Chaplain to the Forces; served in France;
attached to 2nd Canterbury Regiment,
N.Z.E.F.; mentioned in despatches.

*LUTTMAN-JOHNSON, Capt. H. M. ... 1888-92 *a*
Lieut.,Royal West Kent Regiment,December,1914,to May, 1915; Lieut.,R.E.,May,
1915; Capt., R.E., July, 1916; wounded,
October, 1916; mentioned in despatches.

*MACARTNEY-FILGATE, Lieut.-Col.
A. R. P. H. ... ... 1886-9 *Price*
The RoyalWelsh Fusiliers, 3rd Bn. (Res.);
O.B.E. (Military).

MACCARTHY, Midshipman G. ... 1910-15 *Prep.*
Royal Navy; 1917, H.M.S. Collingwood.

MACCOLL, Flight Sub-Lieut. A.J.H. 1909-11 *f*
Royal Navy.

*MACDONALD, Lieut.-Col. I. T. A. 1897-1901 *T*
Royal Army Service Corps; Assistant
Director, Department of Local Resources,
Mesopotamia Expeditionary Force; mentioned in despatches (twice); O.B.E.

*MACGILLYCUDDY, Capt. A. R. N. ... 1901-5 *b*
R.A.M.C., French Base Hospital; M.C.

MACKINTOSH, Lieut. H. S. ... 1912-14 *a*
R.H.A.; 'K' Battery, No. 8 Res. Brigade;
served in France with ' B ' Battery, 83rd
Brigade, R.F.A., 18th Division.

84

†*Macwhirter, Major T. ... 1900-2 *b*
The Gordon Highlanders, 9th (S.) Bn.
(Pioneers); wounded twice; M.C.; killed
on the Arras Front, April 27th, 1917.

*Mair, Capt.(Bt.Major and temp.Lieut.-Col.)
J. A. F. ... ... ` ... 1902-5 *d*
East Yorkshire Regiment; Army Signal
Service; Chief Signal Officer, 11th Corps;
mentioned in despatches; M.C.

Mair, Capt. R. P. ... ... 1899-1904 *d*
Sussex Yeomanry, 1st Bn.; attached to
11th Royal Sussex Regiment; served with
North Russia Expeditionary Force.

Mais, Lieut. S. P. B. ... ... 1913-17 *Master*
Unattached List (T.F.),Sherborne O.T.C.,
1913 to 1917; Tonbridge O.T.C., 1917.

*Malone, Lieut.-Col. C. R. R. ... 1874-6 *a*
Ret. Pay; since September, 1914, was
successively Adjutant, 7th Bn., and 2nd in
Command of 13th Bn., and in Command
of 14th Bn., Worcestershire Regiment,and
15th (S.) Bn. and 16th (Reserve T.) Bn.,
The Hampshire Regiment; reverted to
retired pay, with rank of Lieut.-Col., Nov.
17th, 1917; mentioned for war services.

Mann, R. H. ... ... 1912-17 *d*
Bristol University O.T.C. and No. 1,
R.G.A. Officers' Cadet School,Tonbridge.

†Mansel-Pleydell,Lieut. E.M. ... 1903-5 *f*
The Dorsetshire Regiment; joined 3rd Bn.,
August, 1914; went to France, Jan., 1915,
attached Worcestershire Regiment; killed
at Kemmel, Flanders, March 12th, 1915.

†MARSH, Capt. and Adjt. E. W. H.   1893-7   *a*
Indian Army; 13th Rajputs (The Skek-
hawati Regiment); drowned on the Persia,
December 30th, 1915.

†MARSON, 2nd Lieut. J. C.   ... 1910-13   *d*
1st September, 1914, gazetted to 6th Bn.,
Loyal N. Lancs; was transferred to The
Welsh Regiment, 8th (S.) Bn. (Pioneers);
went to the Dardanelles, June 15th, 1915;
killed at Suvla Bay, August 8th, 1915.

†MARTIN, 2nd Lieut. C. 1894-6   *d*
Coldstream Guards; killed in action on
St. Quentin Ridge, December 1st, 1917.

MARTYN, Lieut. W. W. 1906-7   *a*
Indian Army; served with 2nd Rajputs,
18th Pioneers, and 116th Mahrattas, in
Egypt and Mesopotamia.

*MARWOOD-ELTON, Lieut.-Col. W.   1879-85   *b*
The Welsh Regiment; Commanded 3rd
Bn. (Reserve); Garrison Commander of
The Severn Garrison, also Competent
Military Authority; attached to Labour
Corps, March, 1917; served in France and
Belgium; mentioned in despatches.

MASON, Capt. B. G.   1912-15   *a*
Royal Field Artillery; 407th Battery, 96th
(Army) Brigade; served in France.

*MASON, Lieut. (a./Capt.) I. N.   ... 1907-11   *f*
The Worcestershire Regiment; attached
18th Bn.; M.C.

MASON, Corpl. J. C.   1891-4   *c*
Army Pay Corps.

MASON, Capt. W. M. ... ... 1910-14 *f*
The South Wales Borderers, 2nd Bn.

*MATHEW, Lieut. C. G. ... ... 1908-9 *c*
The Devonshire Regt., 10th Bn.; served
in Salonika; mentioned in despatches.

MATTERSON, Capt. S. K. ... 1890-93 *d*
Army Remount Service; 47th Remount
Squadron; served in France and Egypt.

MATTERSON, Lieut. W. A. K. ... 1888-93 *d*
Territorial Force Reserve.

*MAUNSELL, Capt. F. H. R. ... 1901-6 *a*
The King's Shropshire Light Infantry;
wounded, November, 1914, and (slightly),
October, 1915; mentioned in despatches.

†MAUNSELL, Capt. R. G. F. ... 1904-8 *a*
Royal Engineers (T.F.), 1/7th Field Com-
pany, Hants; drowned, May 4th, 1917,
on the way to Salonika, when the transport,
'Transylvania,' was torpedoed in the
Mediterranean.

*MAY, Surgeon Vice-Admiral Sir A. W.,
K.C.B., K.H.P., F.R.C.S. ... 1868-71 *b*
Late Director-General of the Medical
Department of the Navy; Commander of
Order of Leopold; Order of the Sacred
Treasure (Japan), 1st Class.

MAY, Capt. C. M. N. ... ... 1888-9 *c*
S.A.M.C., South African Contingent.

MAY, Major G. W. G. ... 1896-1900 *d*
The Cheshire Regiment, 3rd Bn. (Res.);
attached Headquarters, Western Command, Chester.

†MAY, Lieut. H. G. ... { 1902-7 *d*
{ 1914 *Master*
The Dorsetshire Regiment, 3rd Bn. (Res.),
attached 1st Bn.; died, March 28th, 1915,
of wounds received at St. Eloi, March 14th.

†MAY, Lieut. T. R. A. ... ... 1913-17 *a*
Royal Air Force; killed in France, August
9th, 1918.

MAYBURY, Cadet M. ... ... 1914-18 *d*
Cambridge University O.T.C.

MAYES, Rev. R. M. ... ... 1898-1900 *b*
S.C.F., Guards' Repôt, Caterham.

MAYO, Capt. C. W. ... ... 1893-8 *a*
The Royal Sussex Regiment, 13th (S.) Bn.
(3rd South Down).

MAYO, 2nd Lieut. J. T. ... ... 1913-17 *c*
The Dorsetshire Regiment.

McCLELLAN, 2nd Lieut. J. F. M. ... 1910-12 *f*
Tank Corps.

McCLELLAN, Capt. N. G. C. ... 1903-8 *a*
The Royal Welsh Fusiliers, 3rd Bn. (Reserve), attached Welsh Regiment.

McCREA, 2nd Lieut. F. W. W. ... 1912-14 *g*
The Devonshire Regiment, 2nd Bn.;
wounded, January 6th, 1918.

*McCULLAGH, Capt. A. C. H., M.D.,
B.S. ... ... 1897-1900 *a*
T.F. (Reserve); D.S.O.

88

*McCullagh, Capt. (a./Lieut.-Col.)
H. R. ... ... 1894-9 *a*
The Durham Light Infantry, 1st Bn.;
served in India till December, 1916; then
with 2nd Bn., in France; 2nd in Command
8th Bn.,The Bedfordshire Regiment, April
to August, 1917; then a./Lieut.-Col. in
Command 2nd Bn., D.L.I.; transferred to
19th Bn., D.L.I., 1918; mentioned in despatches (thrice); D.S.O.

McEnery, E. H. ... ... 1890-4 *T.*
British Red Cross; in France.

†McEnery, Capt. J. A. ... ... 1890-4 *T.&b*
Royal Engineers; O.C. of 54th Co.; landed
in Belgium with Sir Henry Rawlinson's
Division for the relief of Antwerp, and was
killed at Yser, October 26th, 1914.

*McEnery, Major (a./Lieut.-Col.)
R.T. ... ... 1893-8 *T.*
Seistan Field Force; Bt. Lieut.-Col.;
mentioned for war services, India.

†McGowan, 2nd Lieut. J. S. ... 1911-15 *f*
The Devonshire Regiment; June, 1915,
Commissioned to 3rd Bn.; May 20th, 1916,
went to France, attached to 2nd Bn.; killed
at La Boiselle on the Somme,July 1st,1916.

Mein, Bt. Col. J. E. ... ... 1865-7 *a*
Ret. Indian Army; Staff Lieut., G.S.O.,
3rd Grade.

Mercer, Capt. L. E. ... ... 1896-9 *f*
The Dorsetshire Regiment, 3rd Bn. (Res.);
served in France, May, 1917, to October,
1918; retired, December 18th, 1918.

89

MERRIMAN, 2nd Lieut. F. V. ... 1900-6 *a*

Royal Army Medical Corps; War Hospital, Norwich; Censors Staff at Dunkirk.

MERRIMAN, Pte. T. F. ... ... 1904-9 *a*

Royal Army Medical Corps.

MILLER, Sapper A. O. ... ... 1909-12 *T.*

1st Canadian Railway Troops; wounded at Hooge, April 4th, 1916, when serving (as Trooper) with 1st Canadian Mounted Rifles.

MILLER, 2nd Lieut. H. ... ... 1911-13 *T.*

Tank Corps,'C' Company, 4th Bn.; served as Trooper in 1st Dorset (Queen's Own) Yeomanry, in Egypt and Gallipoli, till wounded on September 2nd, 1915; on recovery did home service with 2nd Dorset Yeomanry; gazetted to Tank Corps, January 31st, 1918; served in France from May 29th, 1918.

†MILLIGAN, 2nd Lieut. A. ... 1912-15 *f*

Princess Louise's (Argyll and Sutherland Highlanders); September, 1915, Commissioned to 3rd Bn. (Reserve); kept at Dreghorn as Bombing Officer till he was 19, and went to France in January, 1917, attached to 7th Bn.; died on May 30th, 1917, from wounds received on May 27th, 1917, during the second advance in the first battle of Arras.

MILLIGAN, 2nd Lieut. W. R. ... 1912-17 *b*

The Highland Light Infantry, 1st (Res.) Gr. Bn.

*MOBERLEY, Major and Bt. Lieut.-Col.
A. H. 1893-6   *a*

Royal Garrison Artillery; mentioned in
despatches (thrice); D.S.O.; Military
Order of Savoy (Chevalier); Order of St.
Maurice & St. Lazarus; Légion d'Honneur.

MOBERLY, Corpl. R. E. 1911-15   *g*

Royal Devon Yeomanry, 1st Bn. (T.F).

MOCKETT, Major H. B. 1895-7   *d*

4th (Queen's Own)) Hussars; served in
France; wounded, September 13th, 1914;
incapacitated by illness contracted on Active Service, from December, 1917, to
October, 1918.

MOCKRIDGE, Lieut. A. H. ... 1912-16   *d*

Royal Field Artillery; served in France
with 303rd Siege Battery; and at Bonn
(Germany) with Army of Occupation.

MOLONY, Lieut. J. T. 1908-10   *f*

The Dorsetshire Regiment, 1/4th Bn.(T.);
attached The Oxfordshire and Bucking-
hampshire Light Infantry; served in India
and Mesopotamia.

MONCKTON, Lieut. J. P. 1906-9   *a*

South Nottinghamshire Hussars.

MONKHOUSE, 2nd Lieut. G. A. ... 1899-1901   *f*

The Buffs (East Kent Regiment),1st (F.S.)
Gr. Bn.

*MONRO, Gen. Sir C. C., K.C.B. ... 1871-3   *a*

The Queen's (Royal West Surrey) Regiment ; Commanding 1st Army, B.E.F. ; Commander-in-Chief in India ; A.D.C. General to the King; mentioned in despatches (thrice); Légion d'Honneur(Grand Officer) ; G.C.B., G.C.M.G., G.C.S.I.; Knight of Grace of Order of Hospital of St. John of Jerusalem.

†MONTGOMERIE, Capt. W. G.   ... 1893-4   *a*

The Prince of Wales's Leinster Regiment (Royal Canadians) ; died, October 20th, 1914, of wounds received near Armentières, October 18th.

MOORE, Major C. G. H.   ... 1899-1903   *c*

R.A.M.C. ; mentioned for War Services.

*MOORE, Lieut.-Comdr. H. R.   ... 1895-99 *Prep.*

Royal Navy ; D.S.O.

†MOORE, 2nd Lieut. R. 1907-13   *a*

The Rifle Brigade (The Prince Consort's Own), 10th Bn. ; after several rejections was accepted by Public School Corps ; made Sergt., and went to France at end of 1915 ; transferred to Cadet Corps at Oxford in Spring of 1916 ; gazetted to Royal Sussex in July, 1916 ; transferred to Middlesex Regiment, went again to France, October, 1916, and was transferred to Rifle Brigade ; died in France on August 15th, 1917, from wounds received in action the previous day, at the forcing of the Steenbeek, in front of Langemark.

†Moore, Trooper R, T. ... ... 1907-8 *b*
Royal Wiltshire Yeomanry (Prince of
Wales's Own Royal Regiment) ; drowned
in the Leinster on his way home on leave
October, 1918.

*Moore, Capt. T. ... ... 1897-1900 *a*
Prince Albert's (Somerset Light Infantry),
1/5th Bn. (T.) ; served in Mesopotamia ;
mentioned in despatches.

More, Lieut. R. McL. ... ... 1913-15 *d*
Royal Garrison Artillery ; served with 5th
Siege Battery in France.

Morgan, Lieut. P. R. J. ... 1912-13 *f*
Royal Engineers (T.F.) ; No. 1, Works
Company, Kent Fortress Engineers.

†Moritz, 2nd Lieut. O. F. ... 1898-1903 *c*
Enlisted in R.A.M.C., September 4th,
1914 ; 1915, Commissioned to The Border
Regiment, 10th Bn. ; transferred to Machine Gun Corps (99th) in same year; went
to France, April, 1916 ; killed at Delville
Wood, July 27th, 1916, while trying to
bring up reinforcements for his gun.

*Morrison, Capt. M. J. ... ... 1907-12 *a*
The Durham Light Infantry, 1/5th Bn.
(T.) ; M.C., with two bars.

*Morton, Lieut. C. W. ... ... 1910-14 *b*
The Worcestershire Regt., 4th Bn.; M.C.

Morton, Lieut. R. J. ... ... 1909-14 *b*
The Duke of Cambridge's Own (Middlesex
Regiment), 2/9th Bn. (T), attached 2/10th
Bn. (T.); 14th Squadron Royal Air Force.

MOSER, Capt. H. B. 1897-1900   *a*
The Cheshire Regiment, 9th (S.) Bn.

MOULTON-BARRETT, 2nd Lieut. E.S. 1909-12   *d*
Seaforth Highlanders (Ross-shire Buffs,
The Duke of Albany's); Royal Flying Corps.

MULOCK, Cadet J. S. 1914-17   *f*
Royal Air Force.

*MURRAY, Major E. M. 1893-8   *f*
Special Reserve, 16th Lancers ; served in
Gallipoli, 1915, as Adjutant of 1/2nd
Scottish Horse; in Egypt, 1916; in France,
1917-18 ; mentioned in despatches.

†MURRAY, Major T. F. 1887-91   *a*
The Highland Light Infantry, 1st Bn.
(Indian Expeditionary Force); killed at the
battle of Festubert, December 20th, 1914.

*MUSPRATT, Capt. C. K. 1906-12   *a*
The Hampshire Regiment, 2/7th Bn. (T.);
served in India, December, 1914 ; in
Mesopotamia since September, 1917; mentioned in despatches.

†*MUSPRATT, Capt. K. K. ... 1911-16   *a*
The Dorsetshire Regiment, attached to
R.F.C. ; served in France, 1917 ; M.C. ;   ·
killed flying on duty in Suffolk, March
16th, 1918.

†*MUSPRATT, Capt. T. P. ... 1910-13   *a*
Gazetted to The Worcestershire Regiment,
3rd Bn., in August, 1914 ; went to France,
September 8th, 1914 ; wounded in the first
battle of the Aisne on September 20th,
1914 ; was temporary Capt. from June,

1915, at the battle of Hooge, onwards;
wounded again, April, 1916, on Vimy Ridge;
mentioned in despatches ; M.C. ; died on
May 29th, 1918, of wounds received the
same day, near Rheims.

MYRES, 2nd Lieut. M. C. ... 1913-18 *a*
No. 2, Cavalry Cadet School, and No. 4,
Cavalry Reserve (Dragoons).

*NAPIER, 2nd Lieut. W. ... ... 1903-5 *d*
Royal Army Service Corps; mentioned in
despatches.

*NEWMARCH, Col. B. J., V.D. ... 1871-3 *b*
Australian Army Medical Corps; in command 1st Australian Field Ambulance,
1914; Senior Surgeon, 2nd Australian
General Hospital, 1915; in command 1st
Australian General Hospital, 1915; in
command 3rd Australian General Hospital, 1916; mentioned in despatches;
C.M.G., C.B.E. (Military).

NICHOLLS, Major F. L. ... 1897-1901 *a*
The Welsh Regt., 2/7th (Cyclist) Bn. (T.)

NICHOLS, 2nd Lieut. A. A. P. ... 1908-11 *d*
The Gordon Highlanders, 3rd Bn.

NICHOLS, 2nd Lieut. W. N. ... 1907-10 *g*
Cheshire Regiment.

NICOLLS, 2nd Lieut. R. M. ... 1911-12 *g*
Royal Field Artillery, 53rd Brigade.

*NORTH, Capt. E. S. ... ... 1907-11 *a*
The Royal Fusiliers (City of London Regiment), 3rd Bn. ; mentioned in despatches.

*Northcroft, Lieut. E. G. D. ... 1910-15 *c*
The Bedfordshire Regiment, 5th Bn., and
84th Machine Gun Coy.; seconded to
Machine Gun Corps, May, 1918; served
in France and Salonika; twice wounded;
mentioned in despatches.

†*Northey, Lieut. A. ... ... 1900-4 *f*
The Worcestershire Regiment, 4th Bn.;
mentioned in despatches; killed at Richebourg St. Vaast, October 12th, 1914.

*Notley, Lieut.-Col. W. K. ... 1893-8 *T.*
Commissioner East Africa Police; temp.
Lieut.-Col. Provost Marshal and Officer
Administering Martial Law, B.E.A., from
August 6th, 1914, to January 22nd, 1919;
mentioned in despatches; D.S.O.; Cavalier
Order of St.Maurice and St.Lazarus(Italy).

†Nutter, 2nd Lieut. G. H. E. ... 1913-17 *a*
Machine Gun Corps, December, 1917,
commissioned; March, 1918, went to
France to M.G.C. of 19th Div.; killed at
Beaumetz, France, March 23rd, 1918.

*Nutting, Capt. A. F. ... ... 1904-8 *f*
The King's Royal Rifle Corps, 11 (S.) Bn.;
M.C. and bar.

Nutting, Capt. L. B. ... ... 1900-2 *a*
Remount Service; Asst. Superintendent
Remount Squadrons; served in France,
1915-17.

*O'Hanlon, Capt. G. 1908-*Master*
The Dorsetshire Regiment, 6th (S.) Bn.;
served in France, July, 1915, to October,
1918; 18th and 8th Corps Schools Instructor, April, 1917, to October, 1918; M.C.

OLDNALL, 2nd Lieut. H. R.   ... 1913-16   *g*
The Worcester Regiment, 1st & 5th Bns.;
served in France; gassed at Vimy Ridge.

*OLLIVANT, Major G. B. 1893-4   *a*
12th (Prince of Wales's Royal) Lancers
(Special Reserve); Bt. Major; mentioned
in despatches.

OLIVER, Major J. F.   1890-2   *d*
The Manchester Regiment, 11th (S.) Bn.

OLIVER, Lieut.-Comdr. T. L.   ... 1883-7   *c*
Enlisted in Sportsman's Bn.; invalided
out; joined R.N.V.R., attached R.N.A.S.

†OLLIVIER, Major G. L. 1900-2   *d*
Royal Garrison Artillery, 6th Siege Battery; went to France, September, 1914;
wounded three times; died of wounds in
Hospital, France, January 20th, 1918.

O'MEARA, Lieut.-Col. E. J., F.R.C.S. 1889-92   *T.*
Indian Medical Service.

†OPENSHAW, Capt. G. O. 1904-8   *f*
Royal Army Service Corps; attached 2nd
Division; wounded and taken prisoner,
May 27th, 1918; died of wounds, August
9th, 1918, at Rastatt, Germany.

ORMSBY, Major T.   ...   ... 1884 *Price*
Army Pay Department; Staff-Paymaster.

*OSTLE, Capt. D. W.   1907-10   *a*
Royal Army Service Corps; mentioned
in despatches.

*PADWICK, Surgeon H. B.   ... 1904-8   *d*
Royal Navy ; D.S.O.

PAGDEN, Sub-Lieut. F. L. K.   ... 1908-10 *Prep.*
Royal Navy.

PAGE, Capt. D. C.   1910-12   *c*
Royal Air Force.

PAGE, 2nd Lieut. K. E. 1910-13   *a*
The Duke of Cambridge's Own (Middle-
sex Regiment), 5th Bn. (Special Reserve) ;
wounded in the head at Monchy-le-Preux,
April 27th, 1917; invalided out, May 23rd,
1918.

†PALMER, Sub-Lieut. E. J.   ... 1905-8   *a*
Volunteered, August, 1914, rejected (de-
fective eyesight); joined Friends' Ambulance in France ; gazetted September, 1915,
to Royal Naval Division, 'Nelson' Bn. ;
died on April 27th, 1917, of wounds received on April 23rd, 1917; buried at
Aubigny, France.

PALMER, H. R. C.   1903-6   *a*
Royal Naval Experimental Service ;
Mechanic.

†PALMER, Lieut. L. S.   1906-9   *a*
The Dorsetshire Regiment, 3/4th Bn. (T) ;
attached to 117th Machine Gun Company ;
killed, September 20th, 1917, at Shrews-
bury Forest, France.

PALMER, Lieut. N. L. L.   ... 1912-15   *a*
Royal Horse Artillery, 'Y' Battery; served
in France with 1st Cavalry Division.

98

*Parham, Capt. H. J. 1909-13   *a*
Royal Field Artillery; mentioned in despatches (twice); Croix de Guerre (French).

Parish, Capt. A. B. O. 1906-9   *d*
The Lincolnshire Regiment, 3rd Bn.

Park, Lieut. R. H. M. 1892-7   *d*
Irish Guards.

†*Parry, Lieut.-Col. C. F. P. ... 1884-6   *d*
Royal Field Artillery, 136th Battery; O.C. 34th Brigade, R.F.A.; served in France from November 5th, 1914, to August 20th, 1918; wounded, August 3rd, 1917; mentioned in despatches (four times); D.S.O.; killed, August 20th, 1918.

Parry, Capt. G. P. 1884-6   *d*
Called out during rebellion in South Africa, but found unfit for service, owing to ill-health, the result of service during Boer War.

†*Parry-Jones, Capt. O. G., M.R.C.S., L.R.C.P. 1900-6   *f*
R.A.M.C. (late 2nd Lieut., Reserve of Officers); Special Reserve; attached Lancashire Fusiliers; Lieut., R.A M.C., January, 1915; Capt., May, 1915; France, July, 1915; attached Suffolk Regiment; mentioned in despatches; died of wounds received at Stuff Redoubt, Thiepval, Oct. 29th, 1916.

Parry-Jones, 2nd Lieut. M. B. ... 1912-17   *f*
Royal Garrison Artillery; served in France with 81st Siege Battery.

99

PARRY-JONES, Capt. P. E. H. ... 1906-11 *f*
South Wales Borderers, 5th Bn.; France,
July, 1915; wounded, July 26th, 1916, at
Mametz Wood; Musketry Instructor, 3rd
Bn., S.W.B., April to October, 1917; In-
structor, 19th O.C.B., Pirbright, November,
1917, to November, 1918.

PARSONS, Lieut. C. P. ... ... 1911-15 *d*
Royal Air Force; previously in R.A.M.C.
and The Wiltshire Regiment; served in
India, Mesopotamia and Egypt.

PARSONS, Capt. G. L. ... ... 1887-9 *c*
R.A.M.C.; September, 1915, M.O., Military Hospital, Millbank; December, 1915,
M.O., 30th General Hospital, Medical Expeditionary Force; March, 1916, M.O.,
16th General Hospital, France; July,
1916, M.O., 1st Worcesters, France; October, 1917, M.O., 11th and 19th, Officers'
Cadet Bns., Aldershot; April, 1918, O.C.,
5th Ambulance Train, France.

†PARSONS, Capt. M. H. D. ... 1895-8 *a*
Royal Horse Artillery, 'O' Battery, 8th
Division; killed in action, in France, July
19th, 1916.

*PARTRIDGE, Lieut.-Col. L. ... 1892-7 *c*
Pembroke (Castlemartin) Yeomanry
(T.F.); late 3rd Dragoon Guards; mentioned in despatches; D.S.O.; Order of
the Nile; Légion d'Honneur (Chevalier).

*PARTRIDGE, Major N. H. E. ... 1887-90 *b*
Royal Army Service Corps; served in
France and Italy; mentioned in des-
patches (twice).

PASLEY, 2nd Lieut. R. M. S. ... 1913-17 *d*
Royal Field Artillery.

PATERSON, Lieut. F. S. 1883-7   *b*
Royal Engineers (T.F.); o/c. Signals,
Forth Fortress Coy. R.E.,December, 1918.

PATERSON, 2nd Lieut. H. R.   ... 1912-17   *b*
Royal Field Artillery, 4th ' B ' Reserve
Brigade.

PEDDIE, Major G.   1886-9   *c*
Hyderabad Volunteers.

*PEELE, Lieut. C. R. de C.   ... 1908-10   *b*
55th Coke's Rifles (Frontier Force);
served in Mesopotamia; mentioned in
despatches.

*PELLY, Capt. F. Brian 1903-8   *a*
Royal Navy; attached to 6th Wing
R.N.A.S.; to 66th Wing R.A.F., April
1st, 1918; to 67th Wing, June 23rd, 1918,
for Intelligence Officer's duties; to Army
Council, for Secretarial duties, January
1st, 1919; A.F.C.

*PENDAVIS, Lieut. H. V. 1909-10   *b*
The Oxfordshire and Buckinghamshire
Light Infantry, 5/2nd Bn.; attached Royal
Flying Corps (1915),France and Flanders;
Egypt (1918), as Instructor in War Fly-
ing; mentioned in despatches; D.S.O.

PENMAN, 2nd Lieut. G. G.   ... 1914-17   *d*
Royal Field Artillery.

*PENNEFATHER, Capt. and Adjt. J. B. 1904-9   *c*
The Loyal North Lancashire Regiment,
6th (S.) Bn.; served in Gallipoli and
with Mesopotamia Expeditionary Force
(M.F.O.), 1916 to 1919; wounded, 1916;
mentioned in despatches (twice); O.B.E.

†*Penruddocke, Lieut. C.   ... 1907-10   *b*
The Duke of Edinburgh's(Wiltshire Regiment), 7th (S.) Bn.; rejoined Colours at outbreak of war; wounded at Salonika, November,1917; mentioned in despatches; M.C.; killed in France, October 4th, 1918.

Perrott, 2nd Lieut. T. H. H.   ... 1913-17   *a*
The Worcestershire Regiment.

Peters, Cadet E. L. du T.   ... 1912-15   *f*
Royal Air Force.

Peters, Pte. J. S. du T.   ... 1914-17   *f*
Young Soldiers' Bn., 52nd (Hants Regt.).

Petherick, Lieut. H. L.   ... 1895-7   *d*
Royal Garrison Artillery.

Phillips, Capt. and Adjt. H. S. ...   1900-3   *a*
Indian Army; 27th Light Cavalry.

*Pick, Surgeon Lieut.-Comdr. B. ...   1893-7   *a*
Royal Navy; R.N. Hospital Haslar; mentioned in despatches.

Pigeon, Lieut. J. W.   1902-5   *f*
R.A.M.C.; No. 12, Indian General Hospital, I.E.F.,' D'; Indian Medical Service.

Pim, Flight Cadet I. M.   ... 1913-18   *a*
Royal Air Force.

Pinhey, Lieut. J. W.   ...   ... 1905-8 *Prep.*
Royal Navy; 1914, H.M.S. Australian; 1915, H.M.S. Nottingham, in which ship present at battle of Jutland, 1916, Submarined.

PINHEY, Capt. R. A. 1906-10   T.
The Buffs (East Kent Regiment), 3rd Bn.,
attached 1st Bn.

*PLANT, Major H. F. 1902-6   a
Royal Field Artillery ; H.Q., R.A., 55th
(West Lancs.) Division ; mentioned in
despatches ; M.C.

PLANT, Lieut. L. H. 1903-8   a
Royal Field Artillery ; August 12th, 1914,
gazetted to 11th Battery, 2nd West Lancs.
Brigade ; May, 1915, went to Egypt with
42nd Div. Ammunition Column ; March
4th, 1917, attached Royal Flying Corps ;
July, 1917, R.F.C. Instructor.

PLAYFORD, Lieut. F. D. 1902-4   a
Surrey (Queen Mary's Regiment) Yeomanry (T.F.).

*POOLE, Capt. E. J. E. 1900-2   d
Indian Army ; 46th Punjabis ; M.C.

†*POORE, Lieut.-Col. R. A., D.S.O. 1885-9   f
Royal Wilts Yeomanry (Prince of Wales's
Own Royal Regiment) (T.F.); appointed
to Command of 2/1st Bn., Royal Wilts
Yeomanry, January, 1915 ; appointed 2nd
in Command 2nd Bn. R. Welsh Fusiliers,
and later in Command ; mentioned in despatches; killed in France, Sept. 26th, 1917.

*POPE, Lieut.-Col. W. W. ... 1871-3   b
Royal Army Medical Corps ; C.M.G.

PORTER, Capt. H. J. A. 1875-7   a
The Devonshire Regt., 3rd Bn.; served
from October 2nd, 1914, to June 1st, 1918 ;
then retired.

*POTHECARY, Bt. Major W. F.   ... 1895-9   *a*
The Hampshire Regiment, 5th Bn. (T.)
(late Sergt., 1st Bn., London Rifle Brigade) ; seconded (1917) as Commandant,
Southern Command Bombing School,
Lyndhurst ; D.C.M. (awarded when serving as Sergt. as above).

*POTT, Lieut. W. T. 1898-1903   *a*
9th (Queen's Royal) Lancers (Special Reserve) ; wounded, March 25th, 1918 ; M.C.

POUND, 2nd Lieut. J. V.   ... 1912-17   *c*
Coldstream Guards, 4th Bn.

†POWELL, Lieut. E. L. 1909-13   *d*
Royal Field Artillery ; served in France,
for 18 months, with R.A.S.C., and then
with 'B' Battery, 174th Brigade, 39th
Division, and as Liaison Officer ; killed at
Cachy on April 6th, 1918.

*POWELL, Capt. (a./Major) H. S. ... 1907-11   *a*
Royal Flying Corps ; mentioned in despatches ; M.C.

POWELL, Rev. J. R.   1904-6   *a*
Army Chaplains' Department (attached
15th Bn., London Regiment, Civil Service
Rifles).

POWELL, Pte. R. C.   1911-14   *a*
Honourable Artillery Company.

POWYS, Capt. A. R.   1895-9   *c*
Alexandra, Princess of Wales's Own Yorkshire Regiment, 2/4th Bn. (T.).

*Powys, Sergt.-Major W. E. ... 1902-6 *c*
East African Service Corps; served in
Bowker's Horse (East African Mounted
Rifles) till disbanded; Croix de Chevalier
de l' Ordre de Leopold II.

Prance, Lieut. G. B. S. ... 1910-14 *a*
Royal Field Artillery, 128th Howitzer
Battery, 4th Division; gassed, September
23rd, 1917; discharged, due to wounds
(gas), June 7th, 1918.

Prevost, Cadet. E. J. ... ... 1915-18 *g*
Royal Navy; R.N.C., Keyham; attached
H.M.S. Vivid.

*Prevost, Lieut.-Col. G. H. ... 1883-6 *Price*
Indian Army; Commandant, 87th Punjabis; served in Mesopotamia; mentioned
in despatches (twice).

Prevost, Lieut. W. A. J. ...1912-15 *g*
Royal Field Artillery,401st Battery; served
in France from September 14th, 1916;
wounded.

Priaulx, 2nd Lieut. O. ... ... 1913-17 *b*
Household Brigade, O.T.C., and 1st, and
3rd Bns., Scots Guards.

†Price, 2nd Lieut. E. W. M. ... 1911-14 *b*
The Hampshire Regiment, 3rd Bn. (Reserve); died in France of wounds received
the same day, July 1st, 1916.

Prichard, Pioneer E. C. ... 1910-15 *f*
Royal Arsenal, Woolwich, and Bedford 'A'
Signal Depôt, Royal Engineers.

†PRICHARD, Major R. G. M. ... 1890-4   *c*

1st GlamorganYeomanry (T.F.), attached
Central India Horse, August, 1914; served
in France; wounded there; March, 1918,
went to Palestine and was there killed on
June 7th, 1918.

*PRICHARD, Major W. O. ... 1892-7   *c*

The South Wales Borderers, 1st Bn.;
wounded in France, 1914; mentioned in
despatches.

PRINCE, Lieut. T. 1910-14   *a*

The Royal Sussex Regiment, 2nd Bn.;
served in France.

PRITCHARD, Capt. H. T. ... 1881-2   *f*

LincolnshireYeomanry (T.F.); late King's
Own Scottish Borderers.

PROSSER, Lieut. C. E. G, ... 1910-14   *d*

Royal Garrison Artillery(T.F.); discharged
on account of ill-health, June 28th, 1918.

†PUCKRIDGE, Capt. C. F. H. ... 1908-12   *d*

The Duke of Cornwall's Light Infantry;
served as Private in University and Public
Schools' Corps, September 17th, 1914, to
May 25th, 1915; Commissioned to 3rd Bn.,
D.C.L.I.; went to France September 19th,
1916, attached to 7th Bn.; promoted from
2nd Lieut. to Capt., September 19th, 1916;
killed in action at Ruyaulcourt (between
Bapaume and Cambrai), March 28th, 1917.

*PUCKRIDGE, Capt. H. V. ... 1911-15   *d*

The King's Shropshire Light Infantry;
R.A.F.; taken prisoner, July 1st, 1918;
released and landed in England, December
14th, 1918; D.F.C.

PUGH, Major H. O., D.S.O. ... 1888-9 *Price*
1st Welsh Horse, Yeomanry (T.F.) ; late
Lumsden's Horse.

PUNCHARD, 2nd Lieut. C. ... 1911-14   a
Royal Field Artillery.

PURBFOY, Lieut. T. A. W. ... 1907-12   c
Royal Army Service Corps ; attached
West Yorkshire Regiment.

QUINEY, Lieut. R. C. 1911-14   c
Tank Corps, Depôt Bn., Wool ; served in
France with 16th Bn., The Duke of Cambridge's Own (Middlesex Regiment) and
with 14th Bn.,Tank Corps; twice wounded.

*RABAN, Brig.-Gen. Sir E., K.C.B.   1864-7   a
Royal Engineers ; mentioned for War
Service ; K.B.E.

RADCLIFFE, Lieut. J. C. 1894-6   c
R.N.V.R. ; Asst. Staff Officer to Rear
Admiral, Stornoway, Isle of Lewis; for-
merlyAmbulance driver,British Red Cross,
Dunkirk, September, 1914,to June, 1915.

RADCLIFFE, 2nd Lieut. J. G. B. ... 1914-18   a
Devonshire Regiment, 3rd and 53rd Bns.

*RADCLIFFE, Lieut. W. H. ... 1907-12   a
The Devonshire Regiment,2nd Bn.; served
in France; mentioned in despatches(twice).

*RADCLYFFE, Capt. M. F. ... 1898-1901   a
4th (Queen's Own) Hussars ; served in
France with 10th Reserve Regt.of Cavalry
from August 15th, 1914; twice wounded ;
mentioned in despatches (thrice) ; M.C.

RADCLYFFE, Lieut. R. A. 1905-7   *a*
4th (Royal Irish) Dragoon Guards; served
in France from October 14th, 1915.

RADFORD, Lieut. A. D. 1888-94   *a*
The Devonshire Regiment, 11th (S.) Bn.

RAE, Commissioner E. V. R. ... 1904-9   *a*
Nigerian Land Contingent.

*RALEIGH, Lieut. A. G. 1911-15   *a*
The Leicestershire Regiment, 3rd Bn.;
prisoner of war from March to December,
1918; M.C.

†RAMSAY, Lieut. D. W. 1905-9   *d*
The Sherwood Foresters(Nottinghamshire
and Derbyshire Regiment), 10th (S.) Bn.;
killed in the attack on the International
Trench near Ypres, February 14th, 1916.

†RANSFORD, Capt. C. G. 1894-5   *a*
The South Staffordshire Regiment, 1st
Bn.; went to Belgium with 7th Div. in
October, 1914; three times wounded in
an attack on a wood near Ypres on October
26th, 1914, and died next day in German
hands.

RAWES, Capt. F. A. M. ... 1895-1900   *a*
Royal Air Force; served in France, in
R.F.A., transferred to R.A.F.,April,1916;
on Staff at Air Ministry for six months in
1918.

RAWLINS, Lieut. E. F. 1902-5   *f*
Indian Army; 10th Lancers; Indian Police.

RAY, 2nd Lieut. W. H. B.   ... 1913-17   *a*
The Dorsetshire Regiment,6th Bn.; served
in France ; wounded at Thiepval.

†READ, Lieut. A. B.   1904-10   *f*
Prince Albert's (Somerset Light Infantry),
1st Bn. ; went to France in August, 1914 ;
killed at Crony in Battle of the Aisne,
about September 19th, 1914.

REBBECK, Major T. V. 1901-5   *a*
The Hampshire Regiment, 1/7th Bn.(T.);
served in Egypt from November, 1914, to
1919.

†REEVES, 2nd Lieut. L. 1913-17   *a*
The Hertfordshire Regiment, 1st Bn. ;
Commissioned, December, 1917 ; went to
France, April, 1918 ; was gassed ; attached
1st Bn., The Essex Regiment, in July,
1918; dangerously wounded in an attackon
the 23rd, and died on the 25th August, 1918.

†REID-TAYLOR, Capt. A. A. C.   ... 1889-94   *a*
The Royal Dublin Fusiliers ; 1914,
appointed Commandant at Port Said; Provost Marshall of Intelligence to General
Staff ; later sent to Indian Government to
organise an Arab Force in Mesopotamia,
at Basra ; rejoined his Regiment at the
Dardanelles, and was there killed on June
28th, 1915.

REES-WEBBE, 2nd Lieut. E. H. N. 1913-17   *b*
Royal Marine Artillery, Woolwich, and
Royal Field Artillery.

RENTON, 2nd Lieut. M. J.   ... 1912-18   *b*
Royal Marine Artillery, Woolwich, and
17th Battery, Royal Field Artillery.

*Renwick, Capt. A. E. 1912-14   *a*

Tank Corps ("F" Bn.); served as private
in The London Regiment(London Scottish)
till 1916; wounded November, 1917; M.C.

Reynell, Capt. G. M. ... 1897-1900   *a*

Royal Army Service Corps; Dep. Asst.
Dir. of Supplies, Headquarters of Administrative Services and Departments.

†Richards, 2nd Lieut. J. D. E. ... 1899-1904   *T.*

The Royal Sussex Regiment, 2nd Bn.;
at the outbreak of war he obtained a Com-
mission in the Special Reserve; went to
France, September, 1914, in R.E. Postal
Section; transferred to Sussex Regiment
in January, 1915; became Battalion M.G.
Officer; killed at the Battle of Loos,
September 25th, 1915.

Richmond, Capt. J. A. 1901-5   *b*

The South Staffordshire Regiment; served
with 1st (Central Africa) Bn., King's
African Rifles, 1914, to 1917; from 1918,
at War Office.

*Rickett, Major G. R. ... ... 1911- *{School M.O.}*

R.A.M.C. (T.F.); attached Dorset Yeo-
manry; O.C., Nasiriya Military Hospital,
Cairo; mentioned in despatches (twice);
O.B.E.

Rickman, 2nd Lieut. J. 1887-93   *c*

Protectorate Forces, attached 1st Road
Corps, East Africa.

*RICKMAN, Major (a./Lieut.-Col.)
R. B. 1894-90   *f*
The Sherwood Foresters(Nottinghamshire
and Derbyshire Regiment), 2/5th Bn.(T.);
late Lieut., 3rd Cheshire Regiment ; mentioned in despatches.

RIDOUT, Major C. A. S., M.S., M.B., Lond.,
F.R.C.S. Eng. 1887-94   *T.*
R.A.M.C. (T.F.); 5th Southern General
Hospital, Portsmouth, 1914, to 1916; 29th
Stationary Hospital, Salonika, 1916 to
1917 ; Italy, 1917 to 1918.

RIX, Capt. H. S. 1884-90   *a*
Indian Army ; United Provinces Horse.

*ROBERTS, Capt. A. C. G. ... 1901-4   *d*
The Devonshire Regiment, 3rd, Bn. ;
attached 2nd Bn·; M.C.

†ROBERTSON, Lieut. W. M. ... 1906-10   *f*
The Lincolnshire Regiment, 2nd Bn.;
went to France, August, 1914, as 2nd
Lieut. ; wounded, August 26th ; made
Lieut. in December ; wounded again on
January 24th, 1915, when with 2nd Bn. ;
killed at Bois Grenier, near Armentières,
June 27th, 1915.

†ROBINSON, 2nd Lieut. B. S. ... 1910-13   *d*
Princess Charlotte of Wales's (Royal Berk-
shire Regiment), 2nd Bn. ; passed out of
Sandhurst in May, 1915 ; promoted 1st
Lieut. in November, 1915; killed in action
near Albert, France, July 1st, 1916.

ROBINSON,Major F.H.,M.B.,B.C. 1899-1903   *b*
R.A.M.C., 'A' Force.

ROBINSON, Lieut. R. G. 1910-14   *c*

Machine Gun Corps, 49th Bn. ; wounded at Bourlon Wood, November 23rd, 1917; previously served in 13th, 20th and 14th Bns., The Welsh Regiment, and 121st Machine Gun Company.

ROBINSON, Lieut. S. G. 1913-15   *c*
Royal Air Force.

ROGERS, Lieut. H.   1912-14   *a*
Royal Garrison Artillery; 182nd Siege Battery.

*ROGERSON, Major E. C. 1884-7   *b*
Royal Garrison Artillery; served in France, 1915, to 1917; mentioned in despatches.

*ROMER, Lieut.-Col. F., M.D.   ... 1884-9   *a*
R.A.M.C. ; served in Gallipoli campaign ; mentioned for War Services, 1917; invalided out on account of injuries received on active service, December, 1918.

ROMER, Lieut. R. P.   1910-14   *a*
Royal Air Force; from October 19th, 1914, to June 18th, 1915, was in 9th (S.) Bn., The Royal Dublin Fusiliers.

*ROOM, Capt. L. C. T. 1897-1901   *c*
Royal Marines ; served in Gallipoli ; mentioned in despatches.

ROPER, Capt. J.   1900-4   *a*
The Dorsetshire Regiment, 1/4th Bn. (T.); served in India.

†ROSE, 2nd Lieut. H. P.... ... 1911-15   *f*
Seaforth Highlanders (Ross-shire Buffs,
The Duke of Albany's), 2nd Bn.; passed
out of Sandhurst, January, 1916; went to
France, October, 1916; killed in action at
the Battle of Arras, near Fampoux, April
11th, 1917.

†ROSS, 2nd Lieut. R. C. 1909-12   *b*
The Royal Scots (Lothian Regiment), 2nd
Bn.; missing,presumed killed,August 26th,
1914, in France.

ROUQUETTE, Lieut. L. P. ... 1911-15   *a*
Indian Army; 39th Mountain Battery,
Indian Expeditionary Force.

ROXBY, 2nd Lieut. N. E. M. ... 1895-9   *T.*
Royal Army Service Corps.

RULE, 2nd Lieut. F. G. 1914-18   *d*
Royal Engineers.

*RUSSELL, Capt. G. B. 1910-14   *d*
The Duke of Edinburgh's (Wiltshire Regiment), 1st Bn.; attached 3rd Bn.; D.S.O.

RUSSELL, 2nd Lieut. J. N. ... 1913-18   *a*
The Royal Fusiliers (City of London Regiment), 3rd Garrison Bn.

†RUSSELL, 2nd Lieut. P. A. ... 1903-7   *b*
Lovatt's Scouts; attached Royal Air Force;
killed, April 2nd, 1917, in France.

‡RUTHERFURD, Pte. H. G. G. ... 1902-5   *f*
The Royal Fusiliers (City of London Regiment),10th Bn.; went to France,July,1915;
killed in advance on Pozieres, June, 1916.

RYBOT, 2nd Lieut. F. J. C.   ... 1915-17   *c*
Royal Garrison Artillery.

*SALMON, Lieut.-Col. G. N.   ... 1885-9   *b*
The Rifle Brigade (The Prince Consort's
Own), 4th Bn.; mentioned in despatches
(four times); C.M.G.; D.S.O.; Distinguished Service Medal (America).

SAMLER, Capt. W. H. G.   ... 1909-13   *a*
Prince Albert's (Somerset Light Infantry),
1/4th Bn. (T.); served in Mesopotamia,
Egypt and Salonika.

SAMUELSON, Capt. G. S. ...   ... 1880-3 *Price*
R.A.M.C.; late Capt. Australian A.M.C.

SANCTUARY, Lieut. A. G. E.   ... 1904-10   *a*
Royal Field Artillery; 1st Dorsetshire Bat-
tery, 3rd Wessex Brigade (T.); served in
Mesopotamia.

SANCTUARY, Capt. C. T. 1902-8   *a*
Royal Field Artillery; attached Royal Air
Force.

†*SANDERS, Capt. A. E. 1904-10   *T.*
The York and Lancaster Regiment, 2nd
Bn.; went to France, December, 1914;
gazetted Capt. early in 1915; served
throughout in Ypres salient; mentioned in
despatches; died of wounds received on
May 19th, 1916.

SANDERS, Capt. E. A. 1904-10   *T.*
The Dorsetshire Regiment, 5th (S.) Bn.,
attached 7th (S.) Bn.

SANDERS, W. R.   1904-8   *T.*
London Regiment, 2/17th Bn.

†SAWYER, Capt. R. H. ... ... 1906-8 *b*

Royal Air Force; enlisted in Canada; chosen for a Commission and attached to Artists' Rifles on arriving in England; joined 36th Squadron as a night Pilot on Home Defence; was C.O. at Hylton and Ashington; went to France in February, 1918, in the 100th Squadron—independent Air Force; died on leave, in London, on August 3rd, 1918, of illness.

SAXON Capt. (a./Major) E. ... 1906·11 *j*

Royal Field Artillery; 3rd Cheshire Battery, The Cheshire Brigade (T.); served in France, Egypt and Mesopotamia, with various units; promoted a./Major while commanding 75th Battery,R.F.A.,November, 1918, to January, 1919.

*SAXON, Capt. H. ... ... 1895-99 *f*

The Royal Sussex Regiment; served in France, in the ranks, with the Royal Fusiliers, and, when commissioned, with 9th Bn.,Royal Sussex Regiment; Prisoner of War, March 22nd, 1918; M.C.

†*SAYRES, Lieut.-Col. A. W. F., M.R.C.S., L.R.C.P. ... ... 1882-4 *Price*

R.A.M.C. (T.F.); was in Camp on outbreak of war and volunteering for foreign service went to France as Major of 1st Wessex Field Ambulance(later called 24th) on November 5th, 1914; made Lieut.-Col., January,1916,in Command of 2/1st Wessex; mentioned in despatches; severely wounded by a shell in the trenches on July 17th, 1917, and died of his wounds on October, 10th, 1917.

115

†SCARBROUGH, Capt. R. J.   ... 1894-98   *a*
Devonshire Regiment, 3rd Bn. ; at outbreak of war joined Indian Army Reserve
of Officers on Garrison work in India; came
to England, August, 1915; rejoined Devons
as Capt.,September, 1915; sailed for Egypt,
November, 1916; was attached to 8th Bn.,
Hampshire Regiment ; wounded at Gaza ;
died in Palestine, November 2nd, 1917.

SCOBELL, Capt. W. B. 1901-5   *a*
Royal Berkshire Regiment.

SCOTT, Col. B. 1877-8   *a*
Indian Army.

SCOTT, Col. C. D.   1874-7   *a*
Royal Garrison Artillery; Chief Instructor
in Gunnery,Coast Defences,Scottish(East).

SCOTT, 2nd Lieut. T. A. R.   ... 1913-16   *g*
Royal Engineers.

SCOTT, 2nd Lieut. G. C.   ... 1911-16   *f*
Royal Field Artillery, A/246 Battery.

SCOTT, 2nd Lieut. S.   1912-15   *c*
Prince Albert's (Somerset Light Infantry),
attached 3rd Bn.

SCOTT, Major W. G.   1900-2   *c*
Devonshire Regiment, 2nd Bn., and 284th
Machine Gun Coy. ; wounded in France ;
also served in India (N.W.F.).

†SCOTT-HOLMES, Lieut. B.   ... 1897-1901   *a*
The King's Royal Rifle Corps, 16th (S.)
Bn. (C.L.B.) ; killed in motor accident at
Wandsworth.

SHARLAND, Gunner W. S. C. ... 1905-7 *d*
Australian Field Artillery.

*SHARP, Capt. A. ... ... 1901-3 *b*
Canadian Expeditionary Force; 19th
Alberta Dragoons and Canadian Light
Horse; served in France; M.C.

SHARP, Lieut. H. A. ... ... 1902-3 *a*
The Royal West Surrey (Queen's) Regiment,9th (Reserve) Bn.,in Salonika; transferred to 8th King's Shropshire Light
Infantry; wounded and invalided home
through shell shock.

SHAW, Capt. H. E. ... ... 1894-7 *f*
Royal Air Force; served in France with
7th (S.) Bn.,The Rifle Brigade (The Prince
Consort's Own); invalided out, June, 1916;
Lieut.,R.N.V.R.,August 26th,1916; Capt.,
R.A.F., April, 1918.

SHAW, Lieut. N. L. ... ... 1905-9 *a*
2nd King Edward's Horse (The King's
Oversea Dominions Regiment); served in
France.

†SHAW, Lieut. W. E. ... ... 1902-7 *f*
The King's Shropshire Light Infantry,
2nd Bn.; died, May 31st, of wounds received on March 15th, 1915.

SHEARS, Capt. R. H. ... ... 1907-11 *f*
The King's Shropshire Light Infantry, 1st
Bn.; and Royal Air Force; served in India.

SHETTLE, Lieut.-Col. H. W. ... 1869-74 *Price*
R.A.M.C. (T.F.); Medical Officer, Red
Cross Hospital, Highfield Hall, South-
ampton; died, April, 1919.

SHEWELL, Capt. A. V. 1911-13   c

The Gloucestershire Regiment, seconded
to R.A.F.; served in France; wounded in
air fight, November 17th, 1916; on London
Defence since October, 1917.

†SHIPPARD, Pte. C. N. W.   ... 1905-7   a

1st New Zealand Expeditionary Force;
joined Wellington Infantry Bn., August,
1914; landed at Gallipoli, April 25th, 1915;
transferred to M. G. Corps; wounded,
and sent home; went to France and was
killed at Armentières, July 10th, 1916.

SIMEY, Rifleman P. A. T.   ... 1907-11   f

North Rhodesia Rifles, Rhodesia; Assist.
Commissioner and Justice of Peace for
North Rhodesia.

†SIMMONS, Capt. F. W. 1901-6   f

The Hampshire Regiment; August, 1914,
joined the O.T.C. Camp, Salisbury Plain,
and was commissioned to 2/4th Bn. (T.),
Hants Regiment; December, 1914, went
to India with his Bn.; September, 1915,
promoted Captain at Quetta; April, 1919,
went to Egypt, and then to Palestine; killed
at Nebi Samuil (Mizpah) on November
22nd, 1917, in attack on Jerusalem, having
been previously wounded earlier in the day.

†SIMMONS, Capt. P. E. M.   ... 1907-12   f

The Hampshire Regiment, 1/4th Bn. (T.);
August, 1914, was in Camp with his Bn.
as 1st Lieut.; promoted Capt.; October,
1914, went to India with his Bn.; March,
1915, went to Mesopotamia with his Bn.,
and was killed in attack on Nasiriyeh on
July 24th, 1915.

SIMMONS, 2nd Lieut. V. A. ... 1913-17   *f*
The Hampshire Regiment, 4th Bn.

SIMONDS, 2nd Lieut. R. M. H. ... 1912-16   *a*
Royal Garrison Artillery.

SIMPSON, Lieut. B. Z. 1911-15   *a*
Royal Air Force; equipment officer.

†*SLADE, Major R. B. 1906-8   *d*
Royal Garrison Artillery; joined No. 1
Company, Poole, Dorsetshire (T.), in
August, 1914; went to France and was
transferred to 123rd Siege Battery; mentioned in despatches,1917; killed in France
on July 10th, 1918.

†SLATER, Lieut. T. A. F. ... 1909-13   *d*
The Dorsetshire Regiment, 5th Bn.; missing, presumed killed, between September
25th, 26th, 1916, at Thiepval Ridge.

*SLOMAN, Brig.-Genl. H. S., D.S.O. 1876-9   *f*
mentioned for War Services and in despatches (twice); C.M.G.; Order of Sacred
Treasure.

SMALLWOOD, Lieut. G. Le W. ... 1886-9   *a*
Royal Field Artillery (Special Reserve);
1st Bn. Reserve Brigade, R.F.A.; served
in France, with 38th Division.

†SMITH, Capt. D. G. 1905-9   *a*
Royal Engineers; died of wounds in France,
June 26th, 1916.

SMITH, Brig.-Gen. G. B. ... 1872-7   *f*
Inspector of R.H. and F.A. in India;
Technical Adviser to O.C. Expeditionary
Force in Mesopotamia.

SMITH, Capt. G. W. Melson   ... 1903-7   *c*
Head Quarters, Claims Commission, British Expeditionary Force, June, 1916, to September, 1919.

*SMITH, Bt. Lieut.-Col. H.M., D.S.O. 1884-7   *a*
The King's Shropshire Light Infantry; Commanding 5th (S.) Bn. ; mentioned in despatches.

SMITH, Major J. U.   1903-7   *f*
Royal Field Artillery; 2/4th East Anglian Brigade, 2/2nd Hertfordshire Battery(T.).

†SMITH, 2nd Lieut. L. S.   ... 1910-14   *f*
The Wiltshire Regiment, 1st Bn. ; in August, 1914, joined Honourable Artillery Co., as private ; September 18th, 1914, went to France as signaller with 1st Bn., H.A.C.; January 19th, 1915, given a Commission (in France) in 2nd South Lancashires ; April, 1915, transferred to 1st Bn., Wilts Regiment ; killed accidentally by a hand-grenade, near Ypres, June 13th, 1915.

*SMITH, Capt. N. H.   1905-7   *d*
R.A.M.C.; served with North Russian Expeditionary Force ; Croix de Guerre.

*SMITH, Capt. P.   1898-1903   *f*
R.A.M.C.; Medical Officer, 2nd Irish Guards; severely wounded, November, 1916; mentioned in despatches (twice) ; M.C.

SMITH, Rifleman R. S. 1911-13   *f*
16th County of London Regiment, Queen's Westminster Rifles ; also served with 1st and 3rd Bn. in France.

†SMITH, Capt. V. N. ... ... 1896-8 *c*

Wiltshire Regiment (The Duke of Edinburgh's), 6th Bn.; given Commission at
outbreak of war in Wilts Regiment; March,
1915, promoted Capt.; July, 1915, went
to France; October, 1915, wounded;
February,1916, returned to France; killed
in Regina Trench, before Miraumonte,
France, November 13th, 1916.

SMYTH, A. J. ... ... 1910-14 *b*

Civilian Prisoner; a member of the School,
spending holidays in Heidelberg; interned
at Ruhleben, November 6th, 1914, to 1918.

†SMYTH, Capt. W. H. ... ... 1892-6 *a*

The Devonshire Regiment; Commissioned
to 11th (S.) Bn.,Devons, November, 1914;
January, 1916; transferred unfit for active
service to 1st Garrison Battalion The
Worcestershire Regiment as Musketry
Officer; November, 1917, went to France
with 2nd Bn.,Worcesters; killed in action
at Neuve Eglise, April 17th, 1918.

*SOPPER, Bt. Major (temp. Lieut.-Col.)
F. W. ... ... 1893-8 *f*

18th (Queen Mary's Own) Hussars; mentioned in despatches (thrice), and for war
services.

SOUTHEY, Pte. C. S. ... ... 1906-7 *f*

R.A.M.C.; 27th Field Ambulance, 9th
Division, B.E.F.

SPARKS, 2nd Lieut. A. B. ... 1914-17 *g*

Royal Air Force.

SPENCER, Lieut. J. H. ... ... 1912-16 *a*
The Dorsetshire Regiment, 2nd Bn.;
served with Egyptian Expeditionary Force,
Palestine, October, 1917, to March, 1919;
in India from October, 1919.

SPREADBURY, 2nd Lieut. H. J. H. 1912-15 *c*
Tank Corps.

SPROULE, Lieut. E. R. L. ... 1914-16 *d*
Royal Naval Air Service and Royal Air
Force; wounded, September 4th, 1918;
prisoner of war in Germany, from that
date; reached England, January 5th, 1919.

†*SPURWAY, Lieut. G. V. ... ... 1907-10 *c*
Prince Albert's (Somerset Light Infantry),
9th (S.) Bn.; joined Sportsman's Bn.,
October, 1914; Commissioned to S.L.I.,
1915; transferred to M.G. Corps; went
to France, August, 1916, with 167th M.G.
Coy.; M.C.; killed in the abortive German attack on Arras on March 28th, 1918.

†SPURWAY, 2nd Lieut. R. P. ... 1904-9 *c*
Prince Albert's (Somerset Light Infantry),
9th (S.) Bn.; attached to 2nd Bn., Hampshire Regiment, December, 1914; des-
patched in August, 1915, to Gallipoli
on the Royal Edward, and was drowned
when that ship was torpedoed on August
14th, 1915.

*SQUARE, Major A. H. ... ... 1901-3 *c*
Royal Field Artillery; mentioned in despatches; M.C.

†STACKE, Lieut. O. G. N. ... 1909-12 *c*
The Royal Inniskilling Fusiliers, 2nd Bn.;
killed in France, 1915.

G

†STALEY, Lieut. F. C.   1903-8   *b*
Prince Albert's (Somerset Light Infantry),
5th Bn.(T.); killed in Mesopotamia, March
8th, 1916.

STALLARD, Lieut. G. W.   ... 1913-17   *a*
Royal Air Force.

*STANFORD, Lieut. E. J. 1913-16   *f*
The Wiltshire Regiment, 4th Bn.; served
in France with 7th Bn.; wounded and
awarded M.C., October 18th, 1918.

*STANGER-LEATHES, Major H. E. ...   1891-6   *d*
Indian Medical Service; served in Mesopo-
tamia; mentioned in despatches; October,
1918, appointed Deputy Asst. Director
Medical Services, Southern Command,
Poona.

STARK, 2nd Lieut. M. A. N. W. ... 1911-15   *f*
The King's Shropshire Light Infantry,
9th (S.) Bn., and 11th Leicesters.

STARK, 2nd Lieut. R. G. W.   ... 1906-8   *f*
The King's Shropshire Light Infantry, 5th
(S.) Bn.

*STEPHENS, Major F. A. ...   ... 1885-8 *Price*
R.A.M.C.; served in France, 1914 and
1915; in Macedonia, 1916 to 1919; mentioned in despatches; D.S.O.; Order of
Saint Sava (Serbian).

STEPHENS, Major J. A., T.D.   ... 1885-7 *Price*
Royal Field Artillery, 2nd Dorsetshire
Battery, 3rd Wessex Brigade (T.); invalided out in January, 1918, on account
of ill-health contracted on active service.

STEVENS, Lieut.-Col. A. F. ... 1885-6   *f*
Indian Medical Service; Divisional S.M.O.,
6th Poona Division.

†*STEVENSON, Lieut. L. W. H. ... 1910-14   *b*
The Royal Inniskilling Fusiliers, 9th (S.)
Bn. (Co. Tyrone); M.C.; killed, in the
battle of the Somme, at Thiepval, July 1st,
1916.

STEWARD, Lieut. J. R. O'B. ... 1911-14   *g*
1/1 Lincolnshire Yeomanry (T.F.)

STEWART, (temp.Capt.) E.W. Hylton 1901-5   *a*
Canadian Army Service Corps; 4th Canadian Divisional Train; served in France
and Belgium.

*STICKNEY, Major J. E. D. ... 1895-8   *d*
The York and Lancaster Regiment, 2/4th
Bn.; mentioned in despatches; D.S.O.;
M.C. with one bar.

STILLWELL, Lieut. C. D. ... 1896-8   *f*
Royal Army Service Corps; 36th (Ulster)
Divisional M.T. Company.

*STOCKTON, Lieut. B. H. B. ... 1912-16   *a*
Royal Field Artillery; served with A/75th
Brigade, with Guards' Division, from
November, 1917; afterwards in the Nor-
thern Division, B.A.O., Germany; men-
tioned in despatches; M.C.

STOCKTON, Lieut. H. O. 1908-11   *c*
The Oxfordshire and Buckinghamshire
Light Infantry, 3/4th Bn. (T.).

STONE, 2nd Lieut. G. F. J. P. ... 1913-16   *e*
The Devonshire Regiment, 3rd Bn.

124

STORRS, Capt. K. S., M.B. (T.F.) ... 1882-5   *a*
R.A.M.C.; attached 5th (T.) Bn., Essex
Regiment.

STOTESBURY, Lieut. A. M.   ... 1912-16   *b*
Gloucestershire Regiment.

STRANGMAN, Lieut. H. W.   ... 1903-7   *c*
Royal Field Artillery; 167th Anti-Aircraft
Section, Independent Force, R.A.F.

†STREATFIELD, 2nd Lieut. T. B. M. 1911-16   *a*
The Queen's Own (RoyalWest Kent Regiment); November, 1916, entered Sandhurst; September, 1917, gazetted to Royal
West Kent Regiment, 1st Bn., and went
to France; killed in action near Passchen-
daele, November 7th, 1917.

*STREET, Major (temp.Lieut.-Col.) A. 1885-91   *b*
Royal Army Service Corps; O.B.E.

*STROUD, Col. (temp.Brig.-Gen.) E.J.   1880-6 *Price*
Royal Marine Light Infantry; Com-
mandant Plymouth Division; commanded
1st Bn. in Gallipoli; commanded 2nd
Brigade, Royal Naval Division at the
evacuation of Gallipoli and, subsequently,
in Salonika and in France; commanded
troops in Aegean Islands, 1917, to July,
1918; Military Governor of Lemnos,
Imbros and Tenedos; mentioned in despatches (twice); C.M.G.

STRUCKMEYER, O. K.   1907-12   *f*
Civilian Prisoner; interned at Ruhleben
from November, 1914, to November, 1918.

STUART-PRINCE, Capt. D. ... 1909-14   *a*
Indian Army, Reserve of Officers; attached
Indian Munitions Board.

*STUDD, Capt. T. Q. 1906-7   *d*
Royal Flying Corps; D.F.C.

*SUNDERLAND, Major B. G. E.   1896-1900   *a*
Royal Garrison Artillery; twice mentioned
for war services; O.B.E.; Cavalier Order
of St. Maurice.

†SWABEY, 2nd Lieut. A. M. C. ... 1909-13   *b*
Prince Albert's (Somerset Light Infantry),
3rd Bn.; killed, near Zonnebeke, April 20th,
1915.

SWANWICK, E. D. 1884-90   *f*
Guards Officer Cadet Battalion.

SWEET, Rev. G. C. W. 1904-9   *a*
Chaplain to the Forces in France, 1918-19.

†SWEET, Capt. L. H. 1908-11   *a*
In Expeditionary Force, August, 1914; at
Le Cateau; joined R.F.C., December,
1914; Flight Commander (temp. Capt.),
February, 1916; killed in air combat, June
22nd, in Belgium.

*SYMES, Capt. (a./Major) A. L. ... 1904-7   *b*
Royal Field Artillery; 1/1st Devonshire
Battery, 4th Wessex Brigade (T.); served
in India, September, 1914, to August, 1916;
then in Mesopotamia with 14th Battery,
4th Brigade, R.F.A., 3rd Division, till
April, 1918; afterwards in Palestine and
Egypt with 'A' Battery, 302nd Brigade,
R.F.A., 60th Division; mentioned in
despatches.

126

Symes, Pte. W. E.   1907-8   *a*
Royal Garrison Artillery, 2nd Heavy Brigade; and 448th Agriculture Coy.,Exeter.

*Symonds, Capt. H. S. P.   ... 1903-7   *a*
The London Regiment, 1/7th (City of London) Bn.; served in France; twice wounded; February, 1919, Adjutant 7th (Reserve) Bn., The London Regiment; mentioned for war services.

†Symons, Pte. H. N.   1904-5   *d*
1/13th (Kensingtons) London Regiment, and Divisional Train of the 56th (London) Division; served in France continuously from October, 1914, until killed in action, near Arras, on December 6th, 1917.

Tamplin, Col. H. T., C.M.G., K.C., J.P.   1863-9   *a*
(Ret. South African Defence Forces); Inns of Court Reserve; commanded Fleet Street Volunteers, subsequently merged into City of London Brigade.

*Tancock, Lieut.-Col. O. K.   ... 1877-80   *c*
Indian Army; Indian Mountain Batteries; Commandant 27th Mountain Battery; C.M.G.

*Tayler, Lieut. (a./Capt.) J. R.   ... 1905-9   *c*
The Duke of Edinburgh's (Wiltshire Regiment), 3rd Bn.; mentioned in despatches (twice); M.C.

Tayler, 2nd Lieut. R.   1908-11   *c*
The Dorsetshire Regiment, 3rd Bn.

Tayler, Lieut. S. E.   1912-15   *a*
Indian Army; 2/39th Garhwal Rifles.

TAYLOR, Rev. A. C. ... ... 1863-4 *b*
Senior Chaplain (retired) Government of
India.

TAYLOR, Pte. F. Sherwood ... 1911-16 *g*
Honourable Artillery Company; wounded
in France and discharged unfit, December,
1918.

TAYLOR, Capt. H. H. C. R.
(see REID-TAYLOR).

TAYLOR, Major, The Rev. R. B.,
D.D. ... ... 1884-7 *d*
Canadian Expeditionary Force; 42nd Bn.
(Royal Highlanders of Canada); now
Principal of Queen's University,Kingston,
Ontario.

*TEMPERLEY, Bt. Lieut.-Col. A. C. 1891-6 *a*
The Norfolk Regiment; G.S.O. (1), Fifth
Army; mentioned in despatches (four
times; C.M.G.; D.S.O.

*TEMPERLEY, Major H. W. V. ... 1893-8 *b*
2nd Fife and Forfar Yeomanry (T.F.);
G.S.O. (2); Order of Crown of Roumania;
Order of Kora George; Assistant Military
Attaché, Serbian Army; O.B.E.

TERRY, Major H. C. E. ... ... 1904-9 *d*
Royal Field Artillery; wounded, June,
1917.

†TERRY, Lieut. J. E. ... ... 1904-8 *d*
Royal Flying Corps; died of blood poison-
ing, at Rouen, October 17th, 1917.

128

TESTER, 2nd Lieut. A. F. ... 1903- *Master*
The Queen's Own (Royal West Kent
Regiment), 1/4th Bn. (T.) ; attached
General Staff, India.

THATCHER, Capt. A. F. B. ... 1911-14 *f*
Prince Albert's (Somerset Light Infantry),
2/4th Bn. (T.); attached to 1/10th Gurkha
Rifles.

THOMAS, Lieut.-Col. A. E. ... 1858-62 *a*
Late 7th Dragoon Guards.

THOMAS, Surgeon E. J. F. 1899-1900 *d*
H.M.S. ' Brilliant.'

THOMAS, Gentleman Cadet P. H. ... 1912-15 *d*
Royal Military College, Sandhurst ; invalided out through ill-health.

*THOMAS, Capt. R. C. ... 1898-1902 *c*
Royal Engineers ; M.C.

THORNTON, 2nd Lieut. G. K. ... 1912-17 *b*
Royal Field Artillery, 14th (Res.) Battery.

THORNTON, Midshipman R. H. ... 1914-17 *b*
Royal Navy.

*THURSTON, Lieut.-Col. V. B. ... 1891-5 *d*
The Dorsetshire Regiment ; served in
Cameroon Campaign to May, 1916 ; commanded 9th Bn.,The Lancashire Fusiliers,
in France, October, 1916, to November,
1917 ; invalided ; commanding 4th Bn.
(T.), The Dorsetshire Regiment ; mentioned in despatches (thrice).

TODD, Major A. H. 1900-3   *f*
Royal Air Force (Medical Service) ; O.C.
of the R.A.F. Hospital, Blandford.

TODD, Lieut. C. L. 1911-14   *f*
The Dorsetshire Regiment, 6th (S.) Bn.

TODD-JONES, 2nd Lieut. G. B. ... 1912-16   *a*
Royal Field Artillery ; B/232nd Army
Brigade.

TOOGOOD, 2nd Lieut. H. C. ... 1911-14   *b*
The Norfolk Regiment, 1st Bn.

TORDIFFE, Capt. H. S. W. ... 1881-9   *a*
The Duke of Edinburgh's (Wiltshire Regiment) (Reserve of Officers).

TOWNSEND, 2nd Lieut. P. D. ... 1906-9   *a*
Royal Field Artillery, 2 B. Reserve Brigade, Special Reserve.

*TOZER (a./Capt.) A. 1906-11   *a*
Royal Engineers (Signal Service), attached
to O.C. Signal Section, 17th Corps Heavy
Artillery ; M.C.

TOZER, Capt. G. A. 1893-5   *a*
The London Regiment, 8th (City of London) Bn. (Post Office Rifles) ; Adjutant
8th (Reserve) Bn., April, 1915, to September, 1917 ; Assistant Controller, attached
to American Tank Commission, September, 1917, to February, 1919.

*TOZER, Major J. C. 1904-7   *a*
Royal Army Ordnance Corps ; mentioned
in H.S. despatches.

†TRASK, Lieut. C. W. T. ... ... 1913-16 *a*
Prince Albert's (Somerset Light Infantry);
attached to The Welsh Regiment ; served
in Egypt and Palestine; killed on Western
Front, August 18th, 1918.

TRELAWNY-ROSS, Lieut. A. H. { 1899-1905 *a*
1911- *Master*
Unattached List (T.F.), Sherborne O.T.C.

TRELAWNY-ROSS, Pte. S. M. T. ... 1909-13 *b*
Artists' Rifles, 1/28th (County of London)
Bn.; prisoner of war, in Bayreuth, Bavaria,
March 24th, to December 12th, 1918.

*TRELAWNY-ROSS,Rev.W.T., C.F. 1898-1903 *a*
The Royal Fusiliers (City of London Regiment), 26th Bn.; served in France ; M.C.

TREMAINE, Lieut.-Col. R. ... 1874-6 *c*
Royal Garrison Artillery (Res. of Officers).

TREVOR, Capt. C. P. ... ... 1904-8 *c*
King's Liverpool Regiment, 2nd Bn.;
served on N.W. Frontier, India, 1914, to
1915 ; Mesopotamia, 1916, and France,
1917; 2nd in Command and Temporary
O.C., 12th Bn., The King's Regiment, in
France ; also served with 20th Divisional
Staff; left France, February, 1918, for
India, and served with 2/2nd Gurkhas,
N.W.F. ; commanded column on Kuki
operations, Burma, in January, 1919.

TRUEMAN, Coy. Sergt.-Major T. L. 1906-10 *a*
Volunteer Calcutta Rifles, 1st Bn. ; invalided out.

†TUCKER, 2nd Lieut. A. R. L. ... 1910-12 *c*
The Royal Warwickshire Regiment, 2nd
Bn. (from Unattached List, I.A.); killed
between Fleurbaix and Le Mesnil, December 18th, 1914.

TUCKER, Capt. J. A. C. ... ... 1904-5 *a*
The Dorsetshire Regiment, 1/4th Bn. (T.);
served in Mesopotamia; wounded.

TUCKER, Lieut.-Col. (Hon. Col.) R. E.
V.D. ... ... 1877-81 *c*
The Devonshire Regiment, 2/5th Bn. (T.);
September, 1915, to July, 1916, on active
service in Egypt; October, 1916, to March,
1917, commanded 66th Provisional Bn.;
June, 1917, to May, 1918, Staff appointment with B.E.F., France.

TUKE, 2nd Lieut. A. F. M. ... 1909-13 *c*
Royal Field Artillery; served from 1915,
to 1917, in Ceylon Planters' Rifle Corps;
from April, 1918, in France, in 'A' Battery,
160th Brigade, R.F.A.

†TUKE, 2nd Lieut. A. H. S. ... 1904-10 *c*
The Northumberland Fusiliers, 3rd Bn.;
killed, near Ypres, May 7th, 1915.

TULLIS, Capt. G. D. ... ... 1905-7 *c*
R.A.M.C.; joined as temp. Lieut., December, 1915; Capt., December, 1916; served
with 23rd Division in France and Flanders
and with No. 50 Casualty Clearing Station;
demobilised, December, 1918.

*TURNER, Major W. A. ... ... 1894-8 *d*
The King's (Liverpool Regiment), 6th
(Rifle) Bn. (T.); mentioned in despatches.

†TURRELL, 2nd Lieut. H. G. ... 1911-13   *c*
The Oxfordshire and Buckinghamshire
Light Infantry; wounded, near Passchen-
daele, August 22nd, 1917; died at St.
Thomas' Hospital, November 3rd, 1917.

TURTON, Capt. L. N. ... ... 1883-86 *Prep.*
Royal Navy.

*TURTON, Major M. S. 1887-92   *T.*
Royal Army Ordnance Department;
D.A.D.O.S., 14th Division, Mesopotamia;
served in France, Mesopotamia and Persia;
mentioned in despatches.

TUSON, Fleet Paymaster (Ret.) A. K. 1862-6   *a*
Additional President for the South of
Ireland Coast Guard.

TWEEDY, Major A. C., T.D. ... 1880-3   *c*
Royal Garrison Artillery (T.).

TYSON, Cadet D. ... ... 1914-16 *Prep.*
Royal Navy : 1917, Osborne; 1919, Dartmouth.

VACHELL, Lieut.-Col. H. R. ... 1866-70   *c*
Royal Army Medical Corps (T.F.).

†VACHER, 2nd Lieut. G. H. ... 1908-13   *c*
The Royal Warwickshire Regiment, 2nd
Bn.; killed at or near Zandvoorde, on or
about October 31st, 1914.

VACHER, 2nd Lieut. W. E. ... 1910-14   *c*
The Duke of Edinburgh's (Wiltshire Regiment), 7th (S.) Bn.

VAN DER BŸL, Capt. A. L. M. ... 1908-11   *a*
Cape Garrison Artillery ; Sectional Commander German West Africa Campaign ; served in France with R.F.A.,1915 ; transferred to R.A.F.,1917; Examining Officer, 18thWing, R.A.F.,Headquarters,London.

†VAN GOETHEM, Capt. and Flight-Commander H. E. 1908-11   *a*
Royal Flying Corps, 10th Squadron ; seriously wounded in an aeroplane accident, May 5th,1916; Instructor to Beaulieu Aerodrome, July 5th, 1917 ; killed while instructing a junior officer in flying, July 11th, 1917.

*VAN STRAUBENZEE, Brig.-Gen.,
C. H. C. 1879-81   *d*
Mentioned in despatches (twice) ; C.B.; C.M.G. ; C.B.E.

VEALE, Lieut. A. P. 1904-7   *a*
Royal Engineers, 177th Tunnelling Company ; formerly in 184th Company.

VENNING, Capt. E. G. ... 1898-1904   *f*
The Duke of Cornwall's Light Infantry, 1/4th Bn. (T.) ; served in Egypt.

VERNON, Lieut. A. S. 1913-15   *g*
Royal Army Service Corps ; Siege Park, Rhine Army, Cologne.

VERNON, Major J. B. ... 1899-1900   *b*
Royal Air Force; Vice-Consul at Dunkirk.

†VICARY, Capt. G. D. 1902-3   *d*
The Devonshire Regiment, 5th Bn. (T.); died in Palestine, November 10th, of wounds received November 8th, 1917.

*VICARY, Lieut. J.   1909-11   *d*

The Gloucestershire Regiment, 2nd Bn.;
mentioned in despatches (thrice) ; M.C.
and two bars.

*VILLAR, Capt. P. L.   1904-6   *b*

The South Wales Borderers, 7th (S.) Bn.;
mentioned in despatches ; M.C.

VINCENT, a./Sergt. J.   1908-9   *b*

Royal Engineers, despatch rider ; also
served in 13th Corps Signal Company
(Canadian).

†Vincent, Capt. W.   1878-82   *a*

The Duke of Cornwall's Light Infantry,
3rd Bn. (Reserve) ; attached to 1st Bn.,
Royal Welsh Fusiliers ; killed during the
retreat from Mons, 1914.

†*VINTER, 2nd Lieut. R. B. W.   ... 1909-14   *b*

The Worcestershire Regiment, 6th Bn.
(Reserve) ; M.C. ; killed, October 30th,
1916, between Lesboeufs and Morval.

†*VIZARD, Capt. H. T.   1910-14   *T*.

Royal Field Artillery, 15th Division (Scottish); mentioned in despatches (five times);
M.C. with two bars ; killed, September
1st, 1918, near Arras, by a splinter from
bomb dropped by aeroplane.

VOSPER, Lieut. D.   1907-11   *a*

The Suffolk Regiment, 4th Bn.; transferred to 247th P.O.W. Company ; served
in Gallipoli, Egypt and France.

†Vowler, Capt.(temp. Major)D.F.S. 1910-12   *a*
Nottinghamshire and Derbyshire Regiment, and Machine Gun Corps; died, February 28th, 1919, of pneumonia contracted in Camp at Hazeley Down, Winchester.

Vowler, 2nd Lieut. J. C. G.   ... 1912-17   *a*
Royal Engineers, 19th Corps Headquarters.

†Vowler, Lieut. J. A. G.   ... 1911-14   *a*
The Prince of Wales's Leinster Regiment (Royal Canadians), 3rd Bn. (Reserve), attached Machine Gun Corps; served in France; died of accidental wounds in Netley Hospital, July, 19th, 1917.

*Wade-Gery, Major H. T.   ... 1913-14 *Master*
The Lancashire Fusiliers, 9th (S.) (3rd Salford) Bn.; M.C.

Waithman, Rev. F. W. T.   ... 1892-6   *a*
Chaplain to the Forces, 4th Class; in France and Mesopotamia.

Waithman, Capt. J. C. 1888-93   *a*
The Queen's (Royal West Surrey) Regiment; Supernumerary Company, 2/5th Bn.

*Wakefield, Major (a./Lieut-Col.)
T. M.   1892-5   *a*
Royal Garrison Artillery; mentioned in despatches (twice); D.S.O.

†*Walker, 2nd Lieut. E. B.   ... 1902-7   *f*
The Queen's Own (Royal West Kent Regiment), 1st Bn.; mentioned in despatches; killed on Hill 60, near Ypres, April 18th, 1915.

WALKER, Lieut. R. D. 1911-14   *f*
The Dorsetshire Regiment, 6th (S.) Bn.
(1914 to 1915); Royal Flying Corps (1915
to 1919).

*WALLER, Bt. Lieut.-Col. (temp. Brig.-Gen.)
R. L.   1887-90   *a*
Royal Engineers, 86th Field Company,
21st Division; mentioned in despatches;
C.M.G.

*WALSH, Col. H. A., C.B.   ... 1868-71   *c*
Retired ; Commanding No. 8 District.

†WALTER, 2nd Lieut. W. G. A.   ... 1902-7   *a*
Australian Field Force, 48th Bn.; killed
on the Somme, August 6th, 1916.

†WARD, 2nd Lieut. E. S.   ... 1911-14   *g*
Gentleman Cadet, Royal Military College,
Sandhurst; 3rd Bn., Oxfordshire and
Buckinghamshire Light Infantry; attached
to R.A.F.; missing, presumed killed,
August 10th, 1917.

WARD, Capt. H. G. L. 1910-13   *a*
The Worcestershire Regiment, attached
to 5th Bn. (Reserve) ; served in France
with 2nd and 5th Bns., June,1915, to June,
1918 ; then transferred to Indian Army,
2/102nd King Edward's Own Grenadiers ;
twice wounded.

WARING, 2nd Lieut. R. T. T.   ... 1914-17   *g*
Royal Air Force ; served in France as
pilot with 54th Squadron.

†WARNER, Lieut. A. A. J.   ... 1907-8   *c*
Singapore Defensive Force; and Grenadier
Guards ; killed in France, August 24th,
1918.

WARNER, Capt. C. T. 1904-7   *c*
22nd Punjabis, Double Company Officer;
prisoner, after Siege of Kut-el-Amarah,
from December 5th, 1915, to April 29th,
1916.

†WARNER, 2nd Lieut. C. W. ... 1914-16   *c*
Indian Army; 3rd Skinners Horse; died
of pneumonia at Quetta, October 14th, 1918.

WARREN, Lieut. F. 1892-6   *f*
The King's Royal Rifle Corps, 4th Bn.;
also served with 17th and 20th Bns.; twice
wounded.

*WATERALL, Capt. H. G. ... 1899-1900   *b*
The Prince of Wales's (North Stafford-
shire Regiment), 1st Bn.; mentioned for
War Services.

WATKINS, Corpl. J. R. 1909-11   *d*
4th Royal Irish Dragoon Guards and
Machine Gun Corps Cavalry (1914 to 1919);
served in France.

WATNEY, Capt. C. W. 1895-8   *a*
Indian Army.

*WATNEY, 2nd Lieut. R. G. ... 1910-12   *a*
R.N.R., H.M. Yacht Valiant; D.S.C.

*WATTS, Col. Sir W., K.C.B., C.B.,
   V.D. 1872-4   *b*
The Welsh Regiment; Commanding 13th
(S.) (2nd Rhondda) Bn., also 20th (Re-
serve) (3rd Rhondda) Bn.; and, during
latter part of war, 1st City of London Cadet
Brigade; mentioned in despatches.

*WATTS, 2nd Lieut. T. P. W.   ... 1912-15   *g*
Royal Air Force ; A.F.C.

WAUGH, 2nd Lieut. A. R.   ... 1911-15   *a*
The Dorsetshire Regiment, attached to
Machine Gun Corps ; prisoner from March
28th to November 24th, 1918.

WAYMOUTH, Ridley   ...   ... 1911-14 *Prep.*
Royal Navy ; 1917, H.M.S. Glorious ;
1919, H.M. Destroyer Vanessa, acting in
Baltic.

WEALLENS, Capt. W. R. W.   ... 1910-14   *a*
2/4th Gurkha Rifles ; served in Mesopotamia.

†WEBB, 2nd Lieut. G. T.   ... 1905-7   *f*
Royal Fusiliers ; killed in France, April
18th, 1916.

WEBB, Lieut. J. L. S.   1911-15   *b*
The South Wales Borderers ; 4th Bn.;
served in Mesopotamia ; was on board
Cameronian when torpedoed, April 15th,
1917.

WEBB, 2nd Lieut. M. H.   ... 1909-12   *b*
The South Wales Borderers, 14th (S.) Bn.

WEBB, Lieut. W. E. K.   ... 1909-12   *b*
O.C. 242nd Heavy Siege Battery Ammunition Column on the Somme, France;
1917, wounded ; previously served with
Caterpillar Tractor Depôt, Aldershot, and
as O.C. Transport Experimental School of
Gunnery, Shoeburyness.

WELD, Lieut.-Col. A. E.   ... 1885-9   *b*
Royal Army Medical Corps.

WELLS, Pte. W. A. ... ... 1900-5 *b*
Canadian Expeditionary Force; 1st British
Columbia Regiment.

WEST, 2nd Lieut. F. R. ... 1908-12 *a*
The King's Royal Rifle Corps,15th(S.)Bn.

WESTALL, N. E. H. ... ... 1915-18 *f*
Entered Royal Air Force, Autumn, 1918.

WESTCOTT, 2nd Lieut. G. F. ... 1907-9 *a*
Royal Air Force.

WESTERN, Lieut. J. W. ... ... 1883-9 *a*
R.N.V.R.; Base Intelligence, Admiral's
Office, Queenstown.

WESTLAKE, Cadet B. A. ... 1914-17 *b*
Cavalry Squadron ; Inns of Court O.T.C.

WESTLAKE, Capt. M. E. K. ... 1910-14 *b*
The Northumberland Fusiliers, 7th (S.)
Bn.; posted to Labour Corps, April, 1917,
and served in France from that date.

†WHATELY, Lieut. P. V. V. ... 1911-15 *b*
179th Machine Gun Company, 60th Division ; served in France, Salonika and
Palestine ; killed, December 27th, 1917,
in the defence of Jerusalem.

WHATLEY, Lieut. L. S. ... ... 1895-7 *T.*
Royal Army Service Corps (M.T.).

WHEELER, 2nd Lieut. E. J. ... 1912-16 *f*
Royal Garrison Artillery, 1/1st Lancs.
Heavy Battery, B.E.F.

WHEELER, Lieut. F. O. 1909-14   *b*
Royal Field Artillery, 2/4th East Anglian
Ammunition Column (T.); served in
Mesopotamia.

*WHINNEY, Major H. F. 1892-6   *f*
The Royal Fusiliers (City of London Regi-
ment), 4th Bn.; mentioned in despatches;
D.S.O.; O.B.E.

WHITAKER, 2nd Lieut. R. M. A. ... 1895-9   *b*
The Dorsetshire Regiment, 6th (S.) Bn.

*WHITE, Major R. K.   1895-7   *a*
Royal Army Medical Corps; mentioned
in despatches (twice); D.S.O.

WHITE, Cadet W. S. R. 1914-16   *d*
Bristol University O.T.C.

WHITEHEAD, Lieut. A. 1901-4   *c*
Royal Army Service Corps.

*WHITEHEAD, Major B. 1903-5   *c*
Royal Army Medical Corps (Field Am-
bulance) and D.A.D.M.S. of the 29th
Division, B.E.F., France; M.C.

WHITEHEAD, 2nd Lieut. G. M. ... 1901-2   *b*
Alexandra, Princess of Wales's Own Yorkshire Regiment, 8th (S.) Bn.

WHITELEY, Capt. G. T. 1887-92   *d*
The Cheshire Regiment, 6th Bn.; attached
23rd Bn.

*WHITFORD, Major C. E.   ... 1884-7   *c*
The Duke of Cornwall's Light Infantry,
1/5th Bn. (T.); T.D.

WHITFORD, Cadet E. R.   ... 1914-18   *c*
Membland Hall, Cadet Battalion.

†WHITFORD-HAWKEY, Lieut. A. H. 1913-17   *c*
Royal Flying Corps; killed in action in
the air (North of Bapaume, over the German lines), on May 9th, 1918.

WHITING, Lieut. H. N. 1910-14   *a*
Prince Albert's (Somerset Light Infantry),
2/5th Bn. (T.) ; served in India.

†WHITNEY, 2nd Lieut. T. G.   ... 1911-15   *a*
The Royal Warwickshire Regiment, 3rd
Bn. (Reserve), attached 2nd Bn.; accident-
ally killed at Parkhurst, Isle of Wight,
June 15th, 1916.

WHITTINGDALE, Lieut. J.   ... 1908-13   *T.*
Royal Army Medical Corps; S.R.; served
with British Red Cross, in Russia, 1915
to 1916.

WHITTINGDALE, T. Y. 1910-13   *T.*
Army Pay Corps; discharged, medically
unfit, 1917.

†WHITTINGSTALL, 2nd Lieut. G.H.F. 1907-9   *a*
The Northumberland Fusiliers, 2nd Bn.;
killed in action in France, August 3rd,
1916, when attached to 11th Bn.

WICKHAM, Cadet H. G. L.   ... 1914-18   *a*
Inns of Court O.T.C. (Mounted Detachment).

†WICKINGS-SMITH, B. G.   ... 1901-3   *c*
Drowned on the 'Lusitania,' May 7th, 1915.

WIGHT, Capt. A. J. L. ... ... 1907-12 *b*
The Hampshire Regiment, 2/9th (Cyclist)
Bn. (T.).

*WIGHT, Lieut. C. H. ... ... 1910-15 *b*
The Middlesex Regiment, 18th Bn.; M.C.

†*WILDMAN, Capt. A. H. ... 1903-8 *b*
130th King George's Own Baluchis(Jacob's
Rifles); with the I.E.F. in South Africa;
mentioned in despatches; killed at Maktau,
East Africa, September 14th, 1915.

WILDMAN, Paymaster-Lieut. T. B. 1902-7 *b*
Royal Naval Reserve; Vice-Consul at
Puerto Moutt, Chile; served on H.M.S.
Otranto.

*WILDY, Lieut. C. W. ... ... 1909 *a*
Inns of Court O.T.C., 1915; 2/5th Bn.,
London Regiment, December 25th, 1915;
attached 10th Bn., Duke of Wellington's
Regiment, July, 1917; seconded R.E.
Signals, August, 1918; mentioned in des-
patches.

*WILLIAMS, Major-Gen. G., C.B. ... 1874-6 *a*
Late R.E.; Director General of Military
Works, India; K.C.I.E.; mentioned in
despatches.

*WILLIAMS, Bt. Lieut.-Col. (temp. Brig.-
Gen.) G. C. ... ... 1895-8 *c*
Royal Engineers, 173rd(Tunnelling)Com-
pany; mentioned in despatches (7 times);
Order of St. Stauislaus; C.M.G.; D.S.O.

WILLIAMS, Major N. J. ... 1897-1904 *T.*
Royal Army Service Corps.

WILLIAMS, Lieut. R. W. ... 1909-12 *a*

The East Surrey Regiment; 4th Bn.; served with 8th Bn., in France; July 1st, 1916, wounded; February, 1917, posted to 30th Training Reserve Bn., Brigade and Battalion Lewis Gun Officer; January, 1918, Battalion Lewis Gun Officer with 4th Bn., East Surrey Regiment, till discharged, December, 1918; then appointed Assistant Adjutant, No. 1 Dispersal Unit, Crystal Palace.

WILLIS, Major F. W. ... 1896-1900 *a*

Royal Garrison Artillery, 246 Siege Battery; served in France, 1914-15; in Mesopotamia, 1916 to 1918.

WILLOUGHBY, Capt. J. H. ... 1910-13 *d*

Royal Marine Light Infantry; formerly in 10th Bn., Royal Marine Brigade, Royal Naval Division.

WILLS, Hon. Capt. G. V. P. ... 1903-5 *d*

Royal Field Artillery, 1st South Midland Brigade, 2nd Gloucestershire Battery (T.) (Reserve).

WILSON, 2nd Lieut. E. A. R. ... 1897-1902 *a*

The London Regiment, 3/13th (Princess Louise's Kensington Regiment); previously a rifleman in 9th London Regiment (Queen Victoria's Rifles).

*WILSON, Rev. P. H. ... ... 1896-1901 *a*

Army Chaplain's Department; 22nd Wing, Royal Air Force, from November, 1916; previously 1st Brigade, Scottish Horse; Military O.B.E.; mentioned in despatches.

144

†*Wilson, 2nd Lieut. R. A. ... 1905-9   *a*
The Durham Light Infantry; 4th Bn.
(T.F.), attached 6th Bn.; killed at Estaires,
April 9th, 1918; M.C.

Wilson, Capt. R. H. 1900-4   *a*
Indian Army; 82nd Punjabis; seconded
for service with Frontier Militia; 2nd in
Command, Kurram Militia.

Wilson, 2nd Lieut. R. M. ... 1905-9   *a*
Royal Engineers, Signalling Service;
Motor Cycle Despatch Rider from September
7th, 1914, to January 26th, 1918.

*Winch, Lieut.-Col. A. B. ... 1897-1901   *f*
2nd Dragoons (Royal Scots Greys);
Adjutant 1st Royal North Devon (Hussars)
Yeomanry; O.B.E.

Winch, Major J. G. 1892-7   *f*
1/1st Royal East Kent (Duke of Connaught's
Own)(Mounted Rifles)Yeomanry
(T.F.); attached to Tank Corps; served
in Gallipoli and Egypt; Commanded 3/1st
Royal East Kent Yeomanry, August,1916,
to January,1917; as Capt.,Reserve Household
Bn., at Windsor, January, 1917, to
February, 1918.

Winch, Lieut. T. M. 1885-91   *f*
Royal Air Force.

*Windle, Lieut. B. G. 1912-16   *g*
Royal Air Force; served in France with
102nd Squadron; prisoner of war, 1917;
repatriated, 1918; D.F.C.

†WINN-SAMPSON, 2nd Lieut. A. H.   1901-4   *d*
The Duke of Cambridge's Own (Middlesex
Regiment), 5th Bn. (Reserve), attached
4th Bn. ; killed, July 1st, 1916.

WOOD, Pte. A. D.   1895-9   *T.*
The Royal Fusiliers (City of London Regiment), 18th, 19th, 20th and 21st (S.) (1st,
2nd, 3rd and 4th Public Schools) Bns.;
'B' Coy., 2nd Bn.; invalided out, November, 1914.

WOOD, Pte. R. S.   1914-17   *d*
Artists Rifles, 2nd Bn., and No. 1 Infantry
Officer, Cadet Bn., Near Plymouth.

†WOOD, 2nd Lieut. T. H. H.   ...   1914 *Master*
The Dorsetshire Regiment, 3rd Bn. (Re-
serve), attached 1st Bn.; killed, near St.
Eloi, April 13th, 1915.

WOODFORDE, Sergt. W. H. B. ...   1897-1901   *c*
Malay States Volunteer Rifles.

WOODHAMS, Lieut. J. P.   ...   1897-1900   *d*
The Royal Sussex Regiment, 8th Bn. ;
wounded, April 9th, 1918.

WOODHAMS, Capt. R. E.   ...   1899-1902   *d*
General List, attached to Lands Direc-
torate, Headquarters, Eastern Command.

WOODHEAD, 2nd Lieut. F. C. T. ...   1914 *Master*
Unattached List (T.F.).

*WOODHOUSE, Capt. D. E. M.   ...   1910-14   *a*
The Queen's Own (Royal West Kent Regiment), 7th (S.) Bn.; served in France;
Instructor at 10th Officer Cadet Battalion
from March,1918; wounded four times; M.C.

WOODHOUSE, Lieut.-Col. F. D. ... 1878-81 *Price*
Dorsetshire Regiment, 4th Bn. (T.F.)
(Reserve).

WOODHOUSE, Lieut. (a./Capt.) R. F. 1909-14   *a*
Royal Field Artillery, 3rd Wessex Brigade,
3rd Dorsetshire Battery (T.); served in
India and Mesopotamia with 336th Brigade, R.F.A.

WOODS, 2nd Lieut. L. N. W. ... 1906-7   *a*
Canadian Expeditionary Force, Canadian
Infantry and Light Horse,and Royal Naval
Air Service.

*WOODWARD, Capt. W. H.   1877-1881 *Price*
Nyasaland Field Force; Military Landing
Officer, Chinde, Portuguese East Africa;
Administrative Commandant British forces
at Chinde and acting Naval Transport
Officer, July, 1917, to June, 1919; men-
tioned in despatches.

WREFORD, Lieut. V. S. J. ... 1913-14   *d*
Royal Field Artillery, 2/1st Northumbrian
Brigade; served in Mesopotamia with the
102nd Brigade; invalided out.

*WRIGHT, Capt. C. W. G. ... 1903-5   *f*
Prince Albert's (Somerset Light Infantry);
Staff Capt., Headquarters, No. 4 District;
served in France; M.C.

*WRIGHTSON, Lieut. A. J. H. ... 1896-1900   *a*
Canadian Expeditionary Force; 1st British
Columbia Regiment, 7th Bn.; M.C.

†WYATT-SMITH, Pte. H. H. ... 1912-15   *b*
28th (County of London) Bn. (Artists'
Rifles); died of appendicitis, February
17th, 1916.

†WYATT-SMITH, 2nd Lieut. J. D. ... 1913-17   *b*

Royal Flying Corps; killed in Italy, on March 17th, 1918, owing to an accident to his machine when leaving aerodrome.

*WYLEY, Capt. D. F. H. 1901-2   *a*

Served in India, Mesopotamia and France; Staff Capt.,3rd Echelon,G.H.Q.; D.A.A.G. (Wimereux Record Section); metioned in despatches (thrice); O.B.E.; M.C.

†*WYLIE, Lieut. A. W. 1905-9   *f*

The Lincolnshire Regiment, 2nd Bn.; mentioned in despatches; killed at Neuve Chapelle, March 10th, 1915.

†*WYNNE, Lieut. M. O. M. ... 1906-8   *d*

Royal Field Artillery; mentioned in despatches; killed at Armentières, August 28th, 1915.

YATES, Lieut. R. A. 1913-17   *a*

Royal Air Force; prisoner of War at Rastall.

YEATMAN, Capt. G. D. 1902-4   *a*

The Dorsetshire Regiment, 2nd Bn.; attached Worcester Regiment.

YOUNG, Capt. F. H. McL. ... 1901-2   *T.*

The Gloucestershire Regiment, 1st Bn.

†*YOUNG, Capt. F. S. N. 1894-7   *c*

Royal Army Service Corps; mentioned in despatches; died in hospital at Bagdad, March 1st, 1918.

YOUNG, Lieut. G. A. 1910-14   *c*
The Duke of Edinburgh's (Wiltshire Regiment), 2/4th Bn. (T.); attached 39th Divisional Signal Company; 2nd Division N.W.F.F., India, and 68, Airline Section, E.E.F. (Palestine).

YOUNG, Capt. H. G. K. 1888-94   *a*
R.A.M.C.; served in France, 1916, to 1919, with 17th Division (53rd Field Ambulance and 7th Bn., The York and Lancaster Regiment) and 72nd General Hospital.

*YOUNG, 2nd Lieut. J. H. ... 1901-3   *T.*
Royal Army Service Corps (M.T.); mentioned in despatches (twice); D.S.O.; M.C.; Order of Redeemer.

YOUNG, L.-Corpl. R. K. 1902-6   *a*
Was rejected as medically unfit for British Army and enlisted, as a Private, in U.S.A. Army (Home Service).

Roll of Honour.

—

Honeste Defunctorum
Memores Vivamus.

—

Abbott, Lieut. E. J. W.
Adamson, Capt. W.
Alderson, Capt. A. G. J.
Armstrong, Lieut.-Col. C. A.
Awdry, Lieut. W. W.

Bacchus, Capt. W. H. O.
Baker, Capt. C. D.
Baker, 2nd Lieut. G. L. J.
Bamford, Pte. A.
Barnes, Capt. J. E. T.
Barry, Capt. N. J. M.
Battersby, Capt. E. M.
Bawdon, 2nd Lieut. R. H.
Bayly, 2nd Lieut. V. T.
Bean, Lieut. C. R. C.
Beckton, Lieut. H.
Benbow, Pte. J. L.
Benison, 2nd Lieut. E. W.
Bennett, Sergt. B. C.
Bennett, Lieut. M. P.
Bennetts, Flt. Sub-Lieut. E. A.
Betts, Flt. Sub-Lieut. C. C.

Blair, 2nd Lieut. G. Y.
Blandford, Pte. C. E.
Blencowe, Capt. E. C. B.
Bligh, 2nd Lieut. E.
Bond, Capt. C. G.
Bowen, Lieut. E. G. A.
Brine, Lieut. E. L.
Broadrick, Major F. B. D.
Brooke, Capt. G. D.
Brown, Lieut. O.
Burgess, 2nd Lieut. P. G.

Campbell, 2nd Lieut. D. G.
Capel-Cure, Capt. B. A.
Card, 2nd Lieut. S. H.
Carr-Ellison, Capt. O. F. C.
Carrington, Capt. H. E.
Caruthers-Little, Capt. A.W. P.
Chatteris, Capt. T. B.
Chichester, Capt. R. G. I.
Clapton, 2nd Lieut. A.
Clark, Capt. H. C.
Clarke, Pte. W. W. E. M.
Clatworthy, 2nd Lieut. T. E.
Collot, 2nd Lieut. T. A.
Crawhall, Lieut. N. G.
Crichton, 2nd Lieut. A. G.
Croft-Smith, Lieut. E. S.
Crosby, 2nd Lieut. A. B. L.
Custance, Surg. G. W. M.

Dandridge, Lance-Corpl. A. P.
Dandridge, Lieut. W. L.
Duckworth, 2nd Lieut. W. H.
Duvall, Rev. (Capt.) J. R.

Eagar, Lieut. D. G.
Eagar, Lieut. F. R.

Edwards, Major B.
Egerton, 2nd Lieut. B. R.
Elliott, 2nd Lieut. E.
Elliott, 2nd Lieut. W. E.
Ellis, Major C. A.
Elsmie, Lieut.-Col. G. E. D.

Fenn, Lieut. E. J. P.
Findlay, Capt. R. de C.
Fitch, 2nd Lieut. D.
Foley, Pte. E. B.
Folliott, 2nd Lieut. J.
Forrest, Lieut. E. A. A.
Fraser, 2nd Lieut. V. A. D.
Freund, Corpl. E. W. T.
Frost, 2nd Lieut. A. C.
Frost, Lieut. J. J.

Gerrard, Capt. P. N.
Gibbons, 2nd Lieut. J.
Goldsmith, Lieut. H. M.
Graham-Montgomery, Capt. G. J. E.
Gray, 2nd Lieut. G. E. M.
Gray, Capt. H. M.
Grierson, Lieut. S. V.
Grove, 2nd Lieut. P. C.
Groves, Corpl. J. S.
Groves, Lance-Corpl. R. E.
Gunning, Lieut. J. W.
Gwyther, Corpl. P. H.

Halliday, 2nd Lieut. C. G. R.
Hampton, Rifleman W.
Hay, Capt. G. W.
Herbage, Pte. S. H. W.
Hicks, Col. R. F.
Hodges, 2nd Lieut. H. B.
Hodgson, Lieut. R. E.

Holmes, 2nd Lieut. B. R. G.
Hooper, 2nd Lieut. L. J.
Hoskins, 2nd Lieut. F. D.
Hyland, 2nd Lieut. H. B.

Jackson-Taylor, 2nd Lieut. J. C.
Janasz, 2nd Lieut. J. G. G.
Jeffreys, Lieut. W. S.
Jenkins, Lieut. R. B.
Jesson, Major R. W. F.

Kendle, Major R. H.
Kestell-Cornish, Capt. R. V.
Kidner, Corpl. F. E.
King, 2nd Lieut. E. W.
Kitson, 2nd Lieut. E. G. T.

Lacey, 2nd Lieut. E. S.
Large, Capt. H. E.
Larnder, Lieut. E. M.
Leeds, 2nd Lieut. J. S.
Legge, Capt. R. G.
Leigh, 2nd Lieut. H. G. T.
Limbery, Capt. C. R.
Limbery, Capt. K. T.
Llewellin, 2nd Lieut. W. M. J.
Lloyd, Lieut. G. L. B.
Lott, Lieut. J. C.
Luard, Lieut.-Col. E. B.

Macwhirter, Major T.
Mansel-Pleydell, Lieut. E. M.
Marsh, Capt. E. W. H.
Marson, 2nd Lieut. J. C.
Martin, 2nd Lieut. C.
Maunsell, Capt. R. G. F.
May, Lieut. H. G.
May, Lieut. T. R. A.
McEnery, Capt. J. A.

McGowan, 2nd Lieut. J. S.
Milligan, 2nd Lieut. A.
Montgomerie, Capt. W. G.
Moore, 2nd Lieut. R.
Moore, Tr. R. T.
Moritz, 2nd Lieut. O. F.
Murray, Major T. F.
Muspratt, Capt. K. K.
Muspratt, Capt. T. P.

Northey, Lieut. A.
Nutter, 2nd Lieut. G. H. E.

Ollivier, Major G. L.
Openshaw, Capt. G. O.

Palmer, Sub-Lieut. E. J.
Palmer, Lieut. L. S.
Parry, Lieut.-Col. C. F. P.
Parry-Jones, Capt. O. G.
Parsons, Capt. M. H. D.
Pearson, Cadet. C. R.
Penruddocke, Lieut. C.
Poore, Lieut.-Col. R. A.
Powell, Lieut. E. L.
Price, 2nd Lieut. E. W. M.
Prichard, Major R. G. M.

Puckridge, Capt. C. F. H.
Ramsay, Lieut. D. W.
Ransford, Capt. C. G.
Read, Lieut. A. B.
Reeves, 2nd Lieut. L.
Reid-Taylor, Capt. A. A. C.
Richards, 2nd Lieut. J. D. E.
Robertson, Lieut. W. M.
Robinson, 2nd Lieut. B. S.
Rose, 2nd Lieut. H. P.
Ross, 2nd Lieut. R. C.

Russell, 2nd Lieut. P. A.
Rutherford, Pte. H. G. G.

Sanders, Capt. A. E.
Sawyer, Capt. R. H.
Sayres, Lieut.-Col. A. W. F.
Scarbrough, Capt. R. J.
Scott-Holmes, Lieut. B.
Shaw, Lieut. W. E.
Shippard, Pte. C. N. W.
Simmons, Capt. F. W.
Simmons, Capt. P. E. M.
Slade, Major R. B.
Slater, Lieut T. A. F.
Smith, Capt. D. G.
Smith, 2nd Lieut. L. S.
Smith, Capt. V. N.
Smyth, Capt. W. H.
Spurway, Lieut. G. V.
Spurway, 2nd Lieut. R. P.
Stacke, Lieut. O. G. N.
Staley, Lieut. F. C.
Stevenson, Lieut. L. W. H.
Streatfeild, 2nd Lieut. T. B. M.
Stuart-French (Stuart), Maj. C.H.
Swabey, 2nd Lieut. A. M. C.
Sweet, Capt. L. H.
Symons, Pte. H. N.

Terry, Lieut. J. E.
Trask, Lieut. C. W. T.
Tucker, 2nd Lieut. A. R. L.
Tuke, 2nd Lieut. A. H. S.
Turrell, 2nd Lieut. H. G.

Vacher, 2nd Lieut. G. H.
van Goethem, Capt. H. E.
Vicary, Capt. G. D.

Vincent, Capt. W.
Vinter, 2nd Lieut. R. B. W.
Vizard, Capt. H. T.
Vowler, Major D. F. S.
Vowler, Lieut. J. A. G.

Walker, 2nd Lieut. E. B.
Walter, 2nd Lieut. W. G. A.
Warner, Lieut. A. A. J.
Warner, 2nd Lieut. C. W.
Webb, 2nd Lieut. G. T.
Whately, Lieut. P. V. V.
Whitford-Hawkey, Lieut. A. H.
Whitney, 2nd Lieut. T. G.
Whittingstall, Lieut. G. H. F.
Wickings-Smith, Mr. B. G.
Wildman, Capt. A. H.
Wilson, 2nd Lieut. R. A.
Winn-Sampson, 2nd Lieut. A. H.
Wood, 2nd Lieut. T. H. H.
Wyatt-Smith, Pte. H. H.
Wyatt-Smith, 2nd Lieut. J. D.
Wylie, Lieut. A. W.
Wynne, Lieut. M. O. M.

Young, Capt. F. S. N.

Printed in the United Kingdom
by Lightning Source UK Ltd.
117677UKS00002B/226